AN
extra ORDINARY
LIFE

ISBN: 978-1-61718-009-5

TABLE OF CONTENTS

Chapter One — Psalm 103:11
Six Months to Live 1

Chapter Two — Psalm 147:3
He Calls the Stars by Name 31

Chapter Three — Psalm 16:11
Moon Over Miami 47

Chapter Four — John 14:6
Let Me Know the Truth 69

Chapter Five — Acts 1:8
Speaking in Spanish 87

Chapter Six — Proverbs 14:1
Do You Appreciate What George Does for You? 111

Chapter Seven — Romans 6:4
May I Join You, Daddy? 135

Chapter Eight — Psalm 46:11
Rumors of War 175

Chapter Nine — Ephesians 3:14-15
Happy Anniversary 193

Chapter Ten — 1 Corinthians 3:9
Fertile Ground 215

Chapter Eleven — 1 Peter 2:4-5
Living Stones 239

Chapter Twelve — Proverbs 22:6
A Wise Investment 269

Chapter Thirteen — Hebrews 4:13
Do You Need to Forgive…? 289

Chapter Fourteen — Revelation 2:11
We Overcome! 303

Scan this code with your camera-equipped smartphone to view the introductory video. If you do not have the QR app on your phone, visit your app store and search for **QR code reader.**

ACKNOWLEDGEMENTS

It is only in retrospect that you can see all that has happened and been accomplished while you are going about your ordinary life. Our lives have been defined by our search and study of God's Word. In the midst of this, we now recognize those special people that God put us alongside for part of the journey. The most special of these are our children—Allen, Phillip and Doyle. They are totally committed and dedicated to the Lord. They are men of integrity and high moral character and are a source of joy to us. They lived the stories in this book and have constantly prodded us to "write them down". But life was much too busy to sit and write about our ordinary lives.

Then one day, we met Lee and Donna Synnott. They became convinced that the stories had to be written. Their energy and enthusiasm are contagious. They set about the task of interviewing us and numerous friends and family members. They were tireless in their efforts of pursuing the goal of getting the book in print. Lee is very familiar with the ins and outs of the book publishing world, having served as CEO of Ingram Book Company for a number of years. Their advice and guidance have been immeasurable and their willingness to read and re-read the transcript and give pertinent feedback was priceless. Lee and Donna, we thank you for your friendship and your unrelenting work on this project.

After getting many of the interviews transcribed, we stepped into the arena of writing the book. We enlisted the aid of Michael and Bonnie Hines. We were not prepared for the onslaught of soul searching their interviews required. They were determined to squeeze out every thought, opinion and especially every feeling we ever had. Thank you Michael and Bonnie for your invaluable assistance in writing this book and your commitment to details.

Sandra Trail, our very special friend and Attorney, guided us through all the editing and administrative issues. Her skills and diplomacy in these matters have been remarkable.

Several friends read numerous drafts of the book and gave pertinent feedback on the contents and helped decide on the final transcript. Our heartfelt thanks go out to each and every one of you.

George and Betty Jackson

PROLOGUE

A few years ago, we traveled to Israel with a group from World Outreach Church (WOC). At that time, we were able to spend a good deal of time with George and Betty Jackson, founders of WOC, and we got to know them better. It was seeing them in this setting, getting an appreciation for the work they do in Israel, and already knowing the contribution they make in Murfreesboro that made us say, "Wow! These two people are amazing!"

George and Betty are very modest people. They needed a lot of encouragement to write this book. They finally agreed because several people convinced them that their personal testimony would be a benefit to others.

This book is mostly a story about their struggles and willingness to learn. They have learned by doing what God put before them. We think you will agree that they tell it in a very humble and compelling way. Their story shows how an ordinary couple became extraordinary Christ Followers.

What is not in the book is how effective they have been at one-on-one ministry, meeting people at their level of need, without prejudice or judgment. The book's title,

AN (extra) ORDINARY LIFE, is a very good way to describe their behavior and success in helping others. They have opened their home to people who needed shelter and loving care. They have bought groceries and mopped floors and taken care of children and the sick and made so many hospital visits and done things that were way out of the norm of ministry. They were doing these things long before there was a church.

In their veterinarian practice, they cared for the owners first and then their animals. They are models of "what is Christian behavior." And yes, they have been educators as well, but first they are servants. They don't talk about the hundreds of hours they spend each year in counseling, teaching, bible studies, and leading prayer groups. Their energy level continues to be amazing. They have both overcome cancer and seem to shrug off maladies that would stop most people. They are wonderful examples for the rest of us.

George and Betty have become great friends and examples in our lives. They have helped us realize that when God calls you to serve Him, He has no plans for your retirement. We may be retired from our careers, but God gives us work in His Kingdom every day and expects us to be obedient to Him. We get up every day eager to see what God will put before us. Our prayer is that through the examples of George and Betty in this book, you too will find the peace and fulfillment in serving God that we have.

Lee and Donna Synnott

AN
extra ORDINARY
LIFE

ONE

SIX MONTHS TO LIVE

For as high as the heavens are above the earth, so great is his love for those who fear him. **Psalm 103:11 (NIV)**

There is a first step to every journey, but more often than not, your foot falls on the path before you ever realize where it leads. So it was that late spring afternoon in 1965, some thirty thousand feet above the Midwest plains. By now, my journey was eleven days old, a bittersweet blur of conflicting emotions. Yet the more I tried to grapple with the meaning of my feelings, the more I found myself gripped by an ache of the unknown.

I looked out of the airplane window, catching my own reflection in the thick-paned glass. Brown, worried eyes, framed in the latest "Jackie Kennedy" hairstyle, stared back at me.

Time was running out.

Glancing back from the scattered clouds slipping beneath the aircraft wing, I focused on the envelope lying on my lap. Shafts of daylight flashed brightly as they caught the sharp corners of the X-rays that peered darkly through the lip. One by one, I pried the negatives out into the open, fumbling for the written lab report inside.

I really don't know why I kept looking at them. I couldn't read them. I couldn't understand them. But maybe up here in the heavens, held up against the clear, reflected afternoon rays, they might offer some unspoken whisper of hope. Taking a deep breath, I laid them down and studied the diagnosis once more.

With a stolen, sideways glance at my young husband, George, I watched his long legs drift out into the aisle as he shifted his tall frame. To this day, I still remember the title of the book that so captivated his weary gaze: *The Lameness of Horses,* by O. R. Adams, DVM. He looked up, taking off his black-rimmed glasses long enough to rub those penetrating pale blue eyes. He was handsome, determined, and smart. Ironically, he was also just days away from graduating from the University of Missouri's School of Veterinary Medicine. I wished he would put his book down and offer some sort of solution, like he usually did, or at least a few words of hope or reassurance. But he didn't have any answers either. Deep down, I knew as well as he did that there was nothing he could say.

I noticed my hand was shaking as I slid the now-darkened X-rays back into their envelope, firmly out of sight, and allowed my gaze to wander past the checkerboard fields to the horizon beyond and into the bright, sunlit kitchen in Columbia, Missouri, where this journey first began.

• • •

THAT MORNING, I bent down to pull the cherry pie out of the oven, my yellow mitt dipping into the bubbling sauce as I tried hard to balance the weight evenly in both hands. "They should enjoy that," I thought to myself as I carefully set the pie down on the kitchen table and glanced around the room. Everything was in place.

George was halfway through the final day of his National Boards, Allen was at school, and Phillip was staying with my parents, two hundred miles away in the southwest corner of the state. He would be three in June and was getting all the attention an energetic toddler could need, far more, at least, than either of his parents could give him right now.

"Just one more set of exams and we'll finally be through," I sighed as I pulled up a chair, took a sip of water, and imagined seven-year-old Allen's big brown eyes open wide as he walked through the back porch door and caught sight of the pie. The reminders and instructions that had occupied me all morning swiftly vanished from my mind. I picked up a pencil and scribbled four simple words: "I love you. —Mother."

I rose awkwardly, reached for the small suitcase resting by my chair, and checked through it again: dressing gown, a couple of books, and newborn clothes. I had everything I needed for the week. It was time. With one last lingering glimpse of the spotless house behind me, I made my way out into the warm spring sunshine to the baby blue Pontiac outside. It was a car I had always wanted—a gift from George after his grandparents died—bright, new, and open-topped. He had hoped, I guess, that a nice home and a convertible would make the demands of veterinary school easier for his wife to bear—and, in many ways, they did.

I was out of breath by the time I swung the case in through the passenger door, walked around the hood, and slowly sank into the driver's seat. It took a few more minutes of shifting and squeezing to get comfortable enough to drive, my stomach pressed tightly against the steering wheel.

The streets of Columbia were lined with pink and white dogwoods in full bloom, their scent drifting past as the car rolled by. On every corner there were magnificent church buildings, great architectural structures standing stately in the spring sunshine, with their darkened stained glass windows, manicured gardens, and impressive façades. I felt about as carefree as one could feel when just about to give birth by Caesarian. I wasn't scared, only relieved. Tomorrow I would be holding our new baby in my arms.

As I turned onto Broadway, it struck me that North Missouri was beautiful in the spring, but I certainly wouldn't miss the winters! All those extra clothes to put on: snowsuit, gloves, mittens, boots, jackets, and scarves! The previous Christmas, when the family had traveled to Florida for George's job interview, it must have been at least eighty-five degrees outside. I remembered driving the boys to Parrot Jungle in our convertible. We passed down royal palm–lined boulevards and basked in the Florida sun. When George had finished and we returned to Missouri, it was below zero! A few weeks later, when we got the news we were moving, I held Allen and Phillip's hands and we all jumped up and down for joy. I was so looking forward to something different. I could already imagine the view.

By now, I had passed through the center of the city, past the restaurants, the libraries, and the small stores. To the right, I could see the early afternoon sun reflecting off the black, ribbed dome of Jesse Hall, the University of Missouri's landmark building that towered over the city. I had worked there as secretary to the university's vice president our first year in Columbia, the last time I was pregnant. The car climbed the steep hill, slowed by traffic in the bustling junction of College Avenue. To my left, the sun disappeared for a moment under the shadow of the red brick ramparts of Stephen's College. My destination was just half a mile ahead.

In those days, Boone County Hospital was a compact brick facility, comfortably set at the top of the hill, off Broadway, and surrounded by trees. It had an excellent clinical reputation but was struggling to keep up with the expanding local demand. I had thought quite seriously of going back to Kansas City for the birth. I trusted the doctors there, and they had guided me well through the complications that had arisen when I was pregnant with the two older boys. But I didn't want to be away from George for so long—especially not during these final weeks of veterinary school. Besides, the local doctors seemed competent enough. I had made it safely through the pregnancy and was in for a routine Caesarian. From this point on, it was as simple as could be.

I parked the car as close to the entrance as possible and put the keys above the visor for George. Carefully, I slid out from under the wheel, then I reached into the backseat for the suitcase. My feet felt even heavier as I steadied my hands on the driver's door. Just a few more steps! Very soon, I found myself being led down the winding corridors, past the maternity wards and into my own private room.

"That's strange," I thought to myself as I looked around. There was just a single bed and a tiny window. Why was I by myself? There had been at least two of us in the room when I had given birth to Allen and Phillip, and it had actually been quite fun. I chuckled as I remembered one of the girls, who'd had her baby before she came to the hospital, and the laughter that followed when the doctor still charged her for the delivery! I shrugged my shoulders and started unpacking a few of my things, barely making myself comfortable before a doctor walked in.

"I'm Dr. Graftin Smith, a surgeon," he said briskly. I wondered why a surgeon would be in my room.

Dr. Smith seemed like a confident man. He was tall, but not quite as tall as George, and he was upfront and businesslike, with a tinge of impatience in his tone. "How are you feeling, Mrs. Jackson?" he said, his dark eyebrows raised and his forehead furrowed with a well practiced look of concern.

"Why, just fine, Doctor," I replied.

"Mrs. Jackson," he said abruptly, "I have some news I need to give you." I wasn't exactly surprised. I had been in and out of the hospital several times in the past few weeks for X-rays and various other tests. I had begun having trouble with my breasts when I was eighteen. With each pregnancy, I experienced greater levels of bleeding. Once our other two boys were born, however, the discharge ceased. I could tell how much this unsettled my obstetrician, but I knew I had safely carried this baby to full term. His anxiety was misplaced. Once the delivery was over, the bleeding would stop just like before. Then we could all move on.

"Tomorrow, as soon as the baby is delivered," he

continued, interrupting my thoughts, "we are going to have to perform another surgery." My eyes opened wide in alarm.

"Mrs. Jackson," he said, this time a little more gently, "you are aware that you have breast cancer?" There was an uncomfortable silence. I didn't say anything.

"I'm afraid the situation is critical," he added, "and we must intervene immediately."

I was shocked. Even though it was warm in the room, I found myself shivering. I couldn't help but think of how different Dr. Smith's manner was from that of Dr. Baum, the doctor who had delivered both Allen and Phillip back in Kansas City. Maybe I should have gone there for this birth after all!

Suddenly, Dr. Smith had an urgent, anxious look in his eyes that I found quite terrifying.

"Mrs. Jackson," Dr. Smith hesitated. "Are you okay?"

I had lived with this problem for more than ten years. He must be wrong. I was here to give birth. Didn't he realize that once the baby was delivered I would be just fine?

"Look. I understand this is difficult, but I need you to sign this piece of paper giving your consent for us to perform any procedure that we might find necessary." He held out a clipboard and handed me a pen. I took hold of it, my hand shaking.

Except for a few closely typed lines at the bottom of the page, the piece of paper looked blank.

"Right here." He tapped the clipboard with his finger.

I tried hard to focus on the blurred lines of small print that danced before my eyes. Could I trust my life in their hands? I swallowed hard. If I signed that piece of paper, the doctors would be able to do anything! Shaking, I handed the clipboard back to Dr. Smith.

"I'm so sorry, but I really can't make that decision without my husband," I said. "If you don't mind, you'll have to talk to him."

An hour passed before George walked through the door. Exams completed, it was as though the weight of the world had just fallen from his shoulders. I hardly dared break the news.

"I've been looking all over town for you, Betty!" His reproachful tone was betrayed by the laughter in his eyes. "And here you've been lying in bed all this time!"

"I guess the exams went well?" I asked, trying to muster a smile.

A cloud passed over George's eyes. The playful spark so evident a moment before had now completely vanished from view.

"Betty Joyce, what's wrong?!"

I told him what Dr. Smith had said—surprised at how composed my words sounded.

George listened calmly, processing my words in his steady, methodical way. I didn't dare look him in the eyes. I could only imagine what he was thinking. His own mother had died a few days after he was born, and he had been raised for the first two years of his life by his maternal grandparents. Their recent deaths had only reopened old wounds.

After some moments, he broke the silence.

"I don't know what to think," he said finally, unwilling to look me in the eye. "I need to talk to Dr. Ebert."

I let out a huge sigh before I even realized that I had been holding my breath. Dr. Ebert, head of the department of clinical medicine at the veterinary hospital, and his wife, Hazel, had become our mentors and friends. They were kind to the children and gracious to a young married couple with no parents close by to call on for counsel or advice. Sometimes, in the evenings, they would stop by for a piece of pie and we would play bridge.

Yes, Dr. Ebert would know what to do.

George drove the few blocks back to campus as the afternoon was drawing to a close. He found Dr. Ebert's study door open and stood in the doorway, hesitating. The professor was absorbed in a stack of papers, silently reading and marking them with a red pen. He was a large man with a thin white mustache that always made him seem much older than he actually was. A pipe lay on his desk, smoke swirling up to the ceiling. As he stood there watching, George remembered his own grandfather—dead these past four years—and felt a sudden and familiar surge of pain. Granddad Myers was the one person in George's life that he could always depend on for advice. He missed him more than ever; it was an ache that never seemed to go away.

"Come in, Jackson," Dr. Ebert said, looking up, and nodding toward the empty chair squeezed next to the bookcase in the corner. "Have a seat."

George paused and found himself reaching into his top breast pocket to pull out his own pipe—a gift from Granddad Myers. He turned it over in his hand, nervously, too preoccupied with his thoughts to know where to begin.

"Go on," Dr. Ebert urged, holding out an open tin of tobacco. The rich aroma filled the room. George took some gratefully and began packing the moist clumps of coarse strands carefully in the bowl as he relayed the doctor's verdict: They had requested permission to do whatever surgery would be necessary.

Dr. Ebert was a man of few words at the best of times, and he listened attentively now, fingers locked beneath his chin, head slightly bowed as he rocked gently backward and forward in his chair.

"It just seems so rushed, so sudden," George concluded, trying to disguise a hint of fear. "Surely, it's too much stress on her body to have a Caesarian section and a bilateral mastectomy at the same time?" He sat back and held the stem of his unlit pipe while trails of smoke drifted slowly upward from the one still lying undisturbed on the desk.

Dr. Ebert remained quiet as George waited for a response—the sound of his own unanswered question reverberating in the stark silence. This was a building where he was accustomed to getting answers, where the discipline of the veterinary sciences had taught him that even the toughest of conditions had a humane solution— yet now all he could hear was the slow ticking of a nearby clock.

There was a sudden creak as Dr. Ebert turned in his chair. Was he fighting back tears? George couldn't see. Dr. Ebert lifted his gaze to the window behind his desk, looking out over the campus grounds, where young men and women were walking cheerfully back to their dorms, finally through with their classes for the day. His back was still turned as the darkening blue of the late afternoon sky appeared to cast a shadow over the office.

"Someone bigger than we are knows what to do," he said.

There was silence as George waited for the punch line, but none came. That was it.

All of a sudden he began to feel claustrophobic, hemmed in by the bookshelf, with nowhere else to turn. The smoke-filled atmosphere felt stale. Weighed down by the urgency of his question and the lack of a clear response, George quickly thanked Dr. Ebert and left.

The next moment he found himself rushing down the hallway and out into the fresh evening air. He was two hundred yards away before his breathing slackened.

His usually rapid strides slowed as he carefully turned Dr. Ebert's words over in his mind. A minute later, he found himself standing by the convertible, looking up at the same darkening sky.

George had no problem believing there was a God—at least not in theory. He had grown up a traditional Methodist with a strong sense of duty and honor, of right and wrong. He could even conceive of a God who cared for him, for me, for the boys, and for our unborn child. But as for a God who knew what to do?

He wasn't so sure.

And now, everyone was counting on him. Whatever decision he made, he would have to live with it for the rest of his life. There were four blocks now between him and the hospital. Four blocks in which to decide.

"What did Dr. Ebert say?" I questioned as he stepped back into the hospital room and sat down beside me on the bed. George looked at me and hesitated. "I can't really explain," he confessed.

"But," he took a deep breath, "after thinking it over, I think it's going to be too much stress on your body to do it all at once. I wouldn't do that to a cow," he added, "I'm not going to let them do that to my wife."

"Wait a second, George," I said, "I'm no cow!" I knew what he was trying to say, but still!

We were interrupted by the sound of footsteps in the hallway. George swiftly rose to his feet as my obstetrician,

Dr. Pingleton, strode purposefully into the room. Behind him was another surgeon, one I had never met before. They both stood, arms folded, towering over the foot of my bed, eyes intent on George. The dim hospital lighting cast shadows on their faces. "Good evening," Dr. Pingleton began. "I presume Mrs. Jackson has filled you in on her conversation with Dr. Smith?"

"She has," George replied.

"Then we'll begin surgery immediately after the Caesarian section tomorrow . . ."

"Dr. Pingleton," George interrupted, "I have decided . . ." he looked at me, paused, and then turned back to the doctors, "We have decided not to have the surgery right now. We want Betty to recover from the C-section first."

It was not the response the obstetrician or the surgeon had expected to hear, and I saw them glance quickly at each other as they both tried, rather unsuccessfully, to mask the visible shock upon their faces.

"We have one month until I finish veterinary school and we leave for Florida," George added, gaining in confidence as he spoke. "We'll wait until Betty has recovered, have her re-examined, and make a decision then."

"With all due respect, Mr. Jackson," Dr. Pingleton said bluntly, "timing is very significant. As soon as your wife delivers the baby, her hormones will cause the cancer to spread through her whole body. You won't have another opportunity to make this decision!" His voice rose sharply as his frustration began to be evident.

"I want her to have more strength before she has the second surgery," George replied, calmly.

"I know this is a difficult decision," the other surgeon interjected in a kindly voice, glancing firmly at Dr. Pingleton. "We are thinking of your wife here and of doing the best we can for her in this situation. We ask you to please reconsider."

Beneath his glasses, George's blue eyes flashed with icy determination as the three men exchanged heated looks. None of them even so much as looked at me.

Finally, Dr. Pingleton broke the silence. "I would like you to come upstairs with us," he said, taking a different tone as he beckoned to George to follow them into the hallway. "I want to show you something." George started to follow the men, but he stopped suspiciously after a few short steps. "Why?" he asked, his tall frame almost blocking the doctors completely from view. "I have made my decision. What is it you want to show me?"

"I want to show you a girl who wouldn't listen to us," the doctor said slowly. "A few months ago she was in your wife's position . . ."

"No!" George said sternly, cutting him short as he sat down by my bed again. "I have made my decision." I knew these physicians were giving us their very best advice. But I admired George. There was a fire in him, a fire he had caught from his father. I had not quite understood it when we were first married. But it was that same determination that had seen him through veterinary school. Now I could see in his eyes that fire, tempered with the tender-heartedness of his grandfather, and a willingness to stand up for what he believed in, to stand up—for me.

Dr. Pingleton stood in the doorway, hands pushed to either side of the doorframe, exasperated. He made one last effort, looking directly at George. "The woman upstairs is dying now," he said quietly. For the first time, someone glanced at me, but only for a brief second. "Mr. Jackson, you do know that this surgery is your last opportunity to save your wife? If we don't act now, she doesn't have long. She has only six months to live!"

George sat with arms folded, saying nothing as the three men stared at each other. Wearily, the doctors filed out.

George took my hand while I stared straight ahead. I don't know which rushed in first: the despair, the numbness, or the fear.

"I need to get Allen now," George muttered quietly, glancing at his watch. "He's still with the neighbors. Besides, visiting hours are up."

I couldn't even say goodbye. I lay there watching him disappear until several minutes had passed and every hope of him returning had been dashed. I looked around the sterile, stark room, wishing desperately I had a roommate to curb the loneliness, but there was only silence. A short time passed before a nurse walked in, put a sleeping pill on my tongue, and handed me a paper cup filled with water. I wanted her to look at me, perhaps take my hand or tell me it was going to be okay. But she was gone before I could say a word, back to her station in a dizzying whirr of efficiency, and then I was alone again. I had never felt so alone.

I put my hand on my stomach, pressing down. There was so much life in me; I didn't feel sick. Yet there was the doctor's pronouncement: "Six months!" It was unavoidable. No matter how much I tried to deafen my ears to its sting, I couldn't erase it from my mind. I could feel its weight, like a heavy blanket covering my body. And each second of loneliness took me closer to a thought I would never have dared voice out loud: "It is my turn to die." My eyes instantly filled with tears and I groaned out loud, every ounce of strength in me straining to block the emotion inside.

I couldn't tell you that I understood generational patterns, but there was a history in George's family that we didn't talk about much—all the women had died young. His grandfather had lost a sister when he was only fourteen. He had then lost his first wife, Ora, in a horrific accident when their daughter Mildred was only eight— she was engulfed in flames from a kerosene explosion that ripped the kitchen stove apart. Then he had lost Mildred, too: she died of pneumonia just a few days after giving birth to George. I was married to a man who had never known his own mother. Now, was I next in line?

"My children!" I pressed my hand again against my stomach, feeling for the edge of a tiny foot against my skin. I found it. I couldn't hold back the tears as they flowed down, too many to wipe away. My body shook with sobs. How I wanted to come up for air, to rise above the surface, but I was sinking deeper and deeper into despair.

Would my baby ever know me?

These are the moments that you never forget, caught in that dreamlike state between sleep and wakefulness. That's where I was as I lay there that night. My mind was spinning, and no matter how hard I tried to control my thoughts, they always came full circle; it always ended the same.

I was completely alone. Wherever I was heading, I was going on my own.

I sank into a fretful sleep, slipping away from reality, slowly, fearfully . . .

I think I must have blocked the next seven days from my mind, all except for a few brief moments: waking up in the middle of the hallway in unbearable pain, watching the nurses walk up and down on their coffee break. I don't even remember seeing the baby! George told me about him during visiting hours, soon after the delivery: a healthy, beautiful, little boy. We named him Doyle Aaron Jackson.

I do recall standing weakly by the window in my room

waving goodbye to George and my younger sister Glenda as they walked into the parking lot outside. They looked so handsome together. I must have called Glenda at some point to take my place at George's graduation ceremony. She was eighteen—pretty, honest, and so much fun. As I watched them leave, despair lodged even deeper within. "I only have six months left," I reminded myself.

Walking gingerly across the room, I lay down carefully on the bed. George was healthy and handsome, and with his professional education behind him, he would marry again. A thought passed through my mind that I desperately tried to erase. It was something I hardly dared think or speak out loud. *Who would care for the boys and baby Doyle?* Even the thought of George maybe choosing Glenda gave me a sense of relief. I knew she would love them. I turned over awkwardly on my side, with my back to the window, and caught a glimpse of a card that had arrived earlier that day. It was from my older sister Dorothy, a pastor's wife. Embossed on the front of the card was a pink tea rose, the kind that often appeared on the hand-painted china cups my sisters and I loved so much. My eyes fell on the simple phrase beneath the rose.

> *For He who put the stars in place*
> *And rules the land and sea,*
> *It's such a loving little task*
> *To care for you and me!*

I opened the card again.

> Hope you feel more like yourself by now.
> It takes a long time to get through something
> like this.
> Love, Dorothy

Dorothy had become a Christian at eighteen, and it had changed her life. She had stopped dating and changed her clothes, her friends, and her habits. Although I loved and respected my older sister, I wasn't ready to make such a commitment.

And yet, in the midst of my turmoil, there was something about that card that reached me. Still, I didn't understand what it was. I looked again at the scripture printed inside:

> *To proclaim your love in the morning and your faithfulness at night* (Psalm 92:2)

Somehow those were the only words that comforted me that week. They would come to mind in the early hours of the morning and I would find myself repeating them over and over again as I lay awake, crying, in the middle of the night.

> *He who put the stars in place . . .*

• • •

IT WAS A WEDNESDAY. Doyle was one week old, and it was finally time for George to take us home. I looked out at the streets from the backseat. The dogwoods were still in full bloom, the sky was still blue, and there was a beautiful, healthy boy asleep in a baby basket on the seat next to me. Everything seemed so right with the world.

Although the roof of the car was now up to shield the baby from the wind, nothing or no one seemed capable of shielding me. The sunshine, so bright and warming a week ago, was glaring and oppressive to me now, its reflection dazzling my eyes from the windows and mirrors of the passing cars. Once light and airy, the heavens felt like lead. I could find no place of comfort, no place for my heart to rest.

I saw George glancing in the rearview mirror as he drove. He smiled when I caught his gaze, but I just looked away and shut my eyes.

Back home, everything was where I had left it. George and Allen had hardly touched a thing. They had eaten meals with neighbors, friends, and at the hospital. Only a few breakfast bowls, piled neatly in the sink, testified to the fact they had been there at all.

George set the baby basket on the kitchen table. Doyle stirred briefly but soon went back to sleep. "May I get you something to eat before I go?" he asked.

"I'm not really hungry," I said. "Thanks all the same."
I sat by the baby, not knowing what to do next.

"Are you sure you'll be fine?"

I nodded.

George took one more look at me, torn between his
two worlds. He still had responsibilities to complete, duties at the veterinary clinic to finish before graduating. "I'll
come and check on you at lunch," he said gently, and left.

I heard the front door close firmly, and then silence.
The house was so quiet. Allen was at school; Doyle was
fast asleep. I was by myself again. Our acquaintances in
the neighborhood were mostly students and their wives,
and they were all as busy as George. There wasn't anyone I
could think of to call.

I reached out to Doyle, still asleep in the basket, and
touched his cheek, half hoping he would wake up and
need something. But he just sighed, his little chest rising
twice in quick succession as he stirred for a second before
falling back into a contented sleep. I rummaged through
my purse for Dorothy's card, found it, walked over to the
kitchen sink, and put it on the windowsill.

It's such a loving little task
To care for you and me!

I looked at the breakfast dishes and began cleaning out
the sink as I had done every morning to give Phillip a bath
when he was a baby. But Phillip wasn't here either—he

was still with Mother, Daddy, and Glenda.

I stared out the window, wondering if our neighbors would be outside. They were retired—old enough to be the boys' grandparents. Surely, they would like to see the new baby, I thought. I leaned my face against the window, hoping to catch a glimpse of them.

But their house looked silent in the bright morning sunshine, and my eyes drifted to the edge of our backyard. It had never bothered me that there was a cemetery bordering our property. I had always liked it, because it was so quiet and peaceful back there. Besides, George had a mortician's sense of humor. In fact, he had been in the family funeral business before moving to Columbia, and when we were first married, he delighted in telling me stories about the business that really gave me an opportunity to lighten up about the subject.

So it wasn't that I was frightened by the cemetery itself, just by the stark summer sunlight as it fell on the elegant headstones, drawing attention to the phrase I had read so carelessly so many times before: "Beloved wife and mother."

The shrill ring of the telephone pierced through my thoughts.

"Betty, dear, it's Mom." It was George's mother, Cleo. "How are you doing? How's the baby?"

"Fine, fine." As enthusiastically as I could, I described Doyle's features, his light eyes and blonde hair...but I quickly began to run out of things to say.

"Betty." There was a pause at the other end of the phone. "You don't sound like yourself. Are you okay?"

"No, I'm not." I was startled by my willingness to talk. I had asked George not to tell our parents about the cancer, since I knew they would only worry. But once I did, the words tumbled out in a rush. I had barely finished when she told me abruptly that she needed to hang up.

"Betty, don't go anywhere," she insisted. "Stay right by the phone." That was it. Where did she think I would go? I was trapped in a prison as it was, locked inside the impenetrable walls of the doctors' diagnosis.

I sat back down at the kitchen table, fingering Doyle's tiny foot, waiting nervously—not even sure what I was waiting for. Had I made a mistake in telling her? I had always heard that people can act in strange and unpredictable ways when you tell them you are going to die. A few minutes passed before the phone rang again. "Betty! It's me, Mom," she began breathlessly. "Listen, I have contacted the Mayo Clinic. You remember that Dad and I were just there for his heart?"

I didn't say anything.

She continued. "I just talked to the head of OBGYN, and he said that your doctor was right. The hormonal changes will spread the cancer throughout your whole body. Now, write this number down. He wants you to contact him immediately."

I wrote down the number and hung up the phone. Then I took a deep breath and picked it up again, knowing that if I waited just one more minute, I wouldn't have the courage.

"Mrs. Jackson?" said the voice at the other end of the line as soon as I was put through. "We've scheduled surgery for Tuesday morning. You should arrive here late Sunday afternoon."

• • •

THERE WAS A SOMBER, overcast sky the following Sunday morning. We spent the ninety-mile drive to Kirksville in relative silence. George was driving and baby Doyle was asleep. Allen was staring impassively out of the window. I thought of Phillip. We should have been on our way south to my parents in Sarcoxie to bring him home by now. I missed him. Instead, he continued to stay at my parents while I traveled north for surgery. I didn't even know when I would be back . . . or if I would be back.

George pulled the car into the driveway of his parents' house. They had prepared a fine lunch in the formal dining room and had been awaiting our arrival, anxious for Allen and the baby to feel as welcome as possible.

George and Allen went in to eat, but I excused myself. The knot in my stomach wouldn't go away. I walked past the living room, with its beautiful antique furniture,

accented by the dark hardwood beams of their opulent
New England Tudor-style home. I couldn't stay there, so I
went outside and stepped down onto the freshly trimmed
back lawn. Glancing back, I saw the four of them sitting at
the dining room table, heard the faint clink of cutlery, and
saw their heads nodding to the rhythm of conversation.

How easily life would carry on without me!

An hour or so later, we were on our way to the airport
with George's father. Allen came to see us off, sitting in the
back seat next to me. We were scheduled to take a short
flight to Des Moines, Iowa, and from there to Rochester,
Minnesota. We would be traveling all afternoon.

I was holding Allen's hand after we finally cleared the
check-in counter and walked out onto the tarmac toward
the waiting plane. I leaned down to give him one last hug,
and he whispered in my ear. "Please hurry, Mommy," his
voice wavered bravely, "I can't make it much longer without you."

I squeezed him tight.

"I'll be home soon," I said, reassuring him as best I
could, as I held back the tears. George took my arm and we
climbed up the stairs into the aircraft. I turned and waved a
final goodbye before ducking forward to enter the cabin. I
sank down in my seat and pushed my face against the tiny
oval window. Allen was waving, holding his grandfather's
hand. He was almost eight and suddenly looked so grown
up. "Oh, Allen," I thought, "if you only knew."

• • •

I LOOKED DOWN. The manila envelope containing the X-rays had fallen from my lap onto the floor by my feet.

I thought of Allen, waving on the airport runway, getting farther away by the minute. What could I leave him to ease the pain of his loss? What would stand the test of time? I tried looking out of the window again, yet I was unable to forget Allen's face. His sad, brown eyes were fixed in my mind with his words: "Mommy, I can't make it much longer without you." In quick succession, I saw Phillip, with his inquisitive features and happy-go-lucky smile, and then baby Doyle, with his striking blue eyes like his father's.

What could I possibly leave them to help them remember me? Nothing I had done in my life would matter. I had painted some china. I had a fur coat. I had a baby blue Pontiac convertible. But what was any of that worth to three little boys with no mother? I had nothing of value to leave behind.

I glanced over at George, still deep in his textbook, still masking the pain so well. He used to tell me that when he was little, he would set out a picture of his mother on top of his dresser. Whenever he came back to his room, he would find it placed back in the drawer, and he would cry himself to sleep. Is that what would happen to me? Would I just end up being a framed picture in a drawer, unseen and unknown by my boys?

Suddenly, through the black darkness of my closed eyes, a familiar scene popped into my mind. I saw myself driving down Broadway once again, through the heart of Columbia. Behind the dogwood blooms, I saw the Presbyterian church on one corner, the Baptist on another, a Jewish synagogue on yet another—houses of worship that I had driven by every Sunday for four years, on the way to First Methodist. "Why are there so many churches?" I would think to myself. "If there is a God, why can't we all be one?"

My lips began a desperate prayer, a prayer that came from a place deep within me, to a God that I was not sure existed; to a Savior I had not yet met. I knew that whatever I told Allen he would tell his brothers and, once they were old enough, they would believe what he said.

"If there is a God," I whispered softly, just below the steady whirr of the airplane engines, "please let me know the truth, before I die, so that I can tell it to my children."

Scan this code with your camera-equipped
smartphone to view the companion video
for Chapter One. If you do not have the QR
app on your phone, visit your app store and
search for *QR code reader.*

TWO

HE CALLS THE STARS BY NAME

He heals the broken hearted,
and binds up their wounds.
Psalm 147:3 (NIV)

There was a chill in the air as we stepped out of the taxi-cab outside St. Mary's Hospital in Rochester, Minnesota: a strange chill laden with the scent of freshly mown grass and the sound of distant bells. I looked up, my curious eyes drawn to the source of the echoing sounds, but all I could catch were the faint rays of the afternoon sun as they lit up a stone cross that soared high above the imposing red brick façade. All around us, storm clouds were gathering. The sky had taken on an eerie glow.

We walked past two wrought-iron lanterns that stood like sentinels in the half-light. In front of us, I could just make out the familiar-looking figure of a saint, etched in the glass above the entranceway, a halo over his head and a wolf lying passively at his feet.

"Who's that?" I asked softly. There was no reply from

George as he strode on ahead, leaving me lagging eight
or ten paces behind. He bounded up the stone steps to
hold the door open. Tall as he was, his slim silhouette was
dwarfed by the stained-glass paneling that arched overhead. I hesitated: I was in no hurry to enter. I was stalling,
and I knew it.

George turned back and kindly motioned me on, saying softly, "Betty." It took everything in me to keep going
forward.

"Now, go easy on the room service!" he said as we
passed through the teak wood doors into the hushed calm
of the brightly lit lobby. But his attempt to ease the tension
fell flat, drowned by the weight of our emotions.

Inside, everything about the hospital demonstrated the
quiet confidence of its world-class reputation: it was the
jewel in the crown of the famed Mayo Clinic system and
a far cry from Boone County Hospital in Columbia. All
around us, doctors and nurses went about their business
with an air of efficiency, seeming to glide across the grey
squares of polished marble that reflected the soft glow of a
dozen large lamps suspended from the vaulted ceiling.

Within moments, my paperwork was ready.

"You will have to undergo a series of tests across five sep-
arate departments," said the lady at the admissions counter.
"They will start first thing in the morning, so please, try
your best to rest well tonight. As soon as they have collated
the results, you'll be cleared for surgery. Do you have any

questions?"

My mind was full of questions, but I had no idea which to ask, so I simply thanked her and said nothing.

"I suppose you'll need somewhere to stay?" she inquired, kindly, as she handed George a list of local rooms available for families of patients at the clinic. He took the sheet of paper, folded it neatly, and slipped it inside his coat pocket before offering to take me up to my room.

"George, I don't think I'm ready to sleep yet, and it would be nice to see your room," I said. We agreed to walk the short distance across the street together and take a look at the rooms for rent.

"Actually, Mr. Jackson," the nurse interjected, "feel free to have dinner out. Mrs. Jackson is not expected in her room before 8:30 this evening."

I felt a sudden rush of relief. I wasn't ready to go to my room. I wanted to see where George was going to stay. I thought he might choose something totally unsuitable, like the dreary basement apartment he had rented for himself during his first year in Columbia, the year I had stayed with Allen at our home in Kansas City while George completed his pre-veterinary courses. Besides, it would give me some comfort to be able to picture him sinking into his usual effortless sleep. I knew I would be lying awake, otherwise, and I wanted to stay with him as long as possible. I needed his strength.

Outside, the wind had picked up and the rain had

begun to fall before I realized, to my surprise, that I had not brought a coat to Minnesota. I wasn't used to forgetting things.

George noticed me shiver and quickly gave me his jacket.

"You don't have to," I said, as he draped it around my shoulders, but he ignored my protests and squeezed my arm tightly.

Thankfully, the first place we looked was suitable enough: a basement room with access to an upstairs shower and a bed almost long enough for George.

"We'll take it," he said, agreeably, much to my relief. I could feel the day beginning to take its toll and found myself wincing audibly as we climbed back up to street level, my aching body feeling the strain. It was past six-thirty, and I had already been up more than fourteen hours: driving with the boys, saying goodbyes, and flying across the country.

"Let's get a cab," George suggested, clearly recognizing that I was weary.

It wasn't long before we arrived at the grand lobby of the Kahler Hotel, built some forty years earlier to serve those who traveled from far and wide, hoping for a miracle at Mayo Clinic. On one side, I could see the candlelit tables of the hotel restaurant, and on the other, the gleaming gifts on display through the windows of the upscale boutique. I knew George was doing his very best to distract me, and I was willing to let him do so.

"Oh, look, George," I called out, my eye caught by an intricately designed silver biscuit basket in the shop window. I stepped across the lobby to take a closer look. It was brightly offset by the overhead lighting, positioned perfectly to reveal the quality of the craftsmanship. Worked into the silver were beautiful flowers, their stems flowing freely down the sides of the bowl and spreading out underneath to form four delicate feet. The lid was held in place with a simple clasp, which, when opened, would lie flat on the table, exposing the biscuits inside. I knew it would look lovely on our dining room table.

"What is it, Betty?" George said, walking up beside me. One word and he would have reached into his wallet gladly and bought it on the spot. And on any other night—at any other time in my life—I would have given him the opportunity. It was truly beautiful.

But suddenly I was struck by the pointlessness of it all.

"I won't need that," I thought to myself. "I just don't need that kind of thing anymore. I don't have time . . ."

I looked up at George. One look at me and he could tell that the distraction wasn't working.

"Never mind," I said. "Let's go and eat."

We sat in the restaurant in silence: not the awkward silence that precedes a difficult conversation, nor the uncomfortable silence that follows, but an aching silence. There was nothing between us. We had our differences and hurts, but there really wasn't anything left unsaid. And in that bustling hotel dining room that night, we weren't alone. On both sides were others with the same vacant, hollow look in their eyes, trying to ease the pain while trying to cope with what life had presented them.

The meal looked good, but I wasn't hungry. Instead I passed the time rearranging my food on the plate, pushing a lonely vegetable from one side to the other. When I tried to eat, I felt sick to my stomach. I didn't want to squander the moment. I tried to force myself to swallow a few bites, for George's sake more than for my own. Finally, I gave up and a waiter graciously took my plate away.

Before long we were back outside again. Just down from the hotel, we could see the floodlights of the Plummer tower shining like a beacon in the dark night. Across the street stood the modern steel Mayo Building, the many lights from the windows testifying to the untold number of people who, like me, had come to this place looking for a last chance to live.

It was time to go back. There was no point in putting it off anymore. George hailed a passing cab and we traveled the last mile back to St. Mary's in silence.

"Try and get some sleep," George said as he walked me back into the lobby, stopping a moment to put his arms reassuringly around me. "They know what they're doing here." I laid my head against his chest. A nurse waited patiently nearby. "I'll take you to your room when you're ready," she said.

I reluctantly let go. "I'll be back here first thing in the morning," George promised. I took one last look behind me as I walked away. He stood tall and strong, looking down the hallway at me, increasingly distant with each step.

My bed was on the side of the room closest to the door. Beside it, a slender girl with jet-black hair was lying motionless on her side, staring out the window. I was relieved to have someone else in the room with me this time, and I began to slip slowly into a hospital gown, attempting to make conversation as I did.

"Why are you here?" I asked.

There was no response. The girl continued looking straight ahead. The more I stared at the girl's ashen face, the more I realized how sick she must be. I saw the intravenous drip in her arm, the fluids entering her body. I realized, to my surprise, that I feared looking into the eyes of someone who was dying even more than lying in a room on my own.

"I'm having a double mastectomy," I quickly told her. "My surgery's scheduled for Tuesday."

I was beginning to wonder if she was still breathing.

"I had a C-section," I said, trying to make conversation. "My baby's ten days old today." She quickly averted her eyes.

I gingerly climbed into bed, exhausted.

"Have you been here long?" I asked. She was silent. I felt a surge of compassion, mingled with despair. She must have been so beautiful once and yet now . . . no one should have to suffer this alone!

I noticed her water glass was empty, so I eased myself out of bed to refill it for her, putting in a straw to make it easier for her to swallow.

"I start my tests in the morning. Guess I'm a little nervous," I told her.

I lay back in the bed, staring at the clock: 8:55. 8:56. Was Allen asleep yet? Had Doyle taken his bottle? What about Phillip? How was he handling the three weeks without his parents? I thought about George, his feet dangling over the edge of the bed. I knew that once he laid his head on the pillow he would be asleep in seconds. I had always envied him for that. I was the worrier. Sometimes, I would wake up in the night for hours on end. If I couldn't go back to sleep, I would even get up and wash the kitchen floor on my hands and knees. Cleaning the house always made me feel better, and that's what I would do now if I could.

"Where do you go when you die?"

The question came out of nowhere, and I suddenly felt my face flush with embarrassment. I had said it out loud.

"I'm so sorry!" I said, rushing to explain myself. "That just slipped out. I didn't mean to upset you." I peered a little closer at my silent companion. "It's just . . . I was thinking about something. For the last ten years, I have been telling my husband that if I died, I would probably go to hell. He always tells me confidently, 'No, you wouldn't!'

"When I ask him why not, he says"—here I started to mimic George's voice—" 'You're a Methodist.'

"'But, George,' I say, 'I have seen no real change in my life!'"

I leaned halfway up on my elbow, staring intently at the woman, and pushed my hair back. "I'm just not sure I believe him. I mean . . . how do you *really* know? Just because I'm a good Methodist doesn't change me—or make my life any different. Back in Columbia, where we live, you can see all these churches lined up in a row: Methodist, Baptist, Catholic, even a Synagogue. . . ."

There was a sudden knock on the door and I looked up, expecting to see the night nurse. Instead, a middle-aged doctor walked in. He was slightly built, with short, salt and pepper–flecked hair. "Mrs. Jackson," he said kindly, "I'll be seeing you for your first round of examinations. If you don't mind, I would like you to come upstairs with me." He waited patiently.

"Now?!" I was shocked. It was nine o'clock on a Sunday night.

He nodded.

"I'm sorry. I wasn't expecting this," I said apologetically. "I don't even have a bathrobe!" I had forgotten that too.

"I'll tell you what. I'll give you my white jacket," he said, noticing my dismay. He began to take it off as, once more, I swung my legs round and slid off the bed.

"No. You can take mine." The voice came from the corner. My roommate slowly lifted her arm and pointed to a chair. "It's there," she said, her eyes for the first time meeting mine. She knew what lay ahead. I knew that she was trying to help me, offering what little she had left.

"Thank you," I said as I followed the doctor out the door. She smiled weakly in reply.

By the time I came out into the bright corridor, the doctor was several paces ahead of me. He seemed unconcerned about the hour or my struggle to keep up; I followed him up the stairs and down a series of corridors toward the examination suites on the hospital's upper floor. I clutched the robe tighter around me as we went past several rooms that were still in use, and then finally into one of our own. I had started to shiver again.

"Are you cold?" he asked, motioning for me to sit up on the raised exam table in the center of the room.

"No, just nervous."

"Are you sure?" There was a warmth about him: he not only understood how I felt, but he seemed to care about it too.

The doctor began checking my heartbeat and my pulse before drawing a small amount of blood to send to the lab. I felt bad that he was having to work this late, so I started to ask some questions. He had traveled a lot before coming to Mayo Clinic, and now he was here to become more specialized in his field. Exactly what that meant, he didn't say. He wasn't very talkative, but he had a kind and pleasant manner about him. Soon, I became comfortable with the silence as he continued the examination.

It went on until midnight.

Meanwhile, I was half lying, half sitting up, propped up on the angled exam table against a couple of firm, thin pillows. Every now and then, I would look up and see him there, patiently at work. He didn't look hurried or concerned, and his presence was reassuring. I no longer felt so cold.

Finally he broke the silence. "I would like to talk to your husband. Is he here?"

"I think he is probably asleep," I said. "We didn't realize the examination would begin tonight. I have no way of contacting him."

"I would like to talk to your husband as soon as possible," he said simply, but not unkindly.

I sat up straight on the table. There was something in his tone. This doctor was not bothered by trifling details like what time of night it was, he just seemed intent on talking to George.

Why did he want to talk to my husband? Was it worse than we thought?

He went back to his clipboard and began to make more notes. I feared the worst, but when I looked at him, I felt strangely at ease.

Could I hear it for myself?

My heart began to pound, and I closed my eyes. I wanted to wait for George, but the need for an answer—*any* answer—got the better of me. I looked straight at him. "Would you be willing to tell me what you were going to tell my husband?"

The doctor paused, as though that thought hadn't crossed his mind.

"Yes, I can," he simply replied. "You have no cancer."

I began to wonder if I was dreaming, but I could feel the cool starched hospital sheet stretched out over my toes, I could see the faint flicker at the far end of the fluorescent light tubes in the ceiling, and I could hear the doctor's clear and audible voice in my ears.

"Of course, that's only one opinion. You'll have to clear five departments before you can know for sure, but according to my findings, you're going to be okay."

My head was spinning. One day I was dying, the next I was not.

"Are you hungry?" he asked, helping me get up.

"No. Thank you."

"Are you sure?" he persisted. "It would be simple enough to have something sent up to your room."

"No," I insisted. "I'm really not hungry."

Then it dawned on me.

"Did the doctors in Columbia make a mistake? They said if I waited only a few days, I would only have six months to live." I studied his face intently.

"No," he replied calmly.

He walked across the room and patted me on the head.

"Go home and take care of your babies," he said, with a quiet air of authority. "We see this all the time." The doctor walked me back to my room before disappearing down the corridor.

I never saw him again.

Back in the room, it took a moment for my eyes to adjust to the half light. I was still dazed. I folded my roommate's robe and laid it gently on the chair, not wanting to disturb her, before climbing gratefully into bed. I was exhausted, yet I still couldn't sleep.

"How did it go?" The thin voice came again through the silence.

"The doctor said he couldn't find the cancer," I replied.

"I'm really happy for you," she said, straining with each breath. "I never thought you had cancer." I felt so encouraged by her.

"I thought the doctors might have made a mistake," I continued, "but this one says they see it every day."

We lay in the darkness, our beds side by side, unable to see each other, but able to talk for the first time.

"I have been fighting cancer for a year," she began. "I always thought I would make it through in the end. A few days ago, my doctor told me I didn't have much time left. There was nothing more they could do."

"Where's your husband?" I asked, remembering that I had seen a wedding ring on her finger when I first entered the room.

"Home. A few days ago I got in my car and drove a couple of hundred miles straight here. I didn't tell him where I was going." I could hear the hopeless anger in her emaciated voice and was shocked by its sudden strength. "I don't want him to see me die."

I didn't know what to say. She was facing what I had just escaped. Yet I had no idea why I had been spared. What comfort could I offer her?

Early the next morning, I woke up, rehearsing in my mind how I would tell George the news and picturing the look on his face when I did. In the end, it just tumbled out in simple, deadpan words.

"How did you sleep?" he said as he walked in the room shortly after seven.

"They put me through some tests last night," I replied. "The doctor said I have no cancer. He wanted to give you the news himself, but there was no way to reach you."

George looked at me and took a deep breath, closing his eyes for a second. I could see his relief, but it was tempered by the knowledge that another round of tests still lay ahead.

The next two days were filled with a battery of examinations. Each time I left George waiting, and each time I came back with one more department cleared. Perhaps, I thought, we would feel the elation once they told us we could go home. Yet, with each successive result, the sense of anticlimax grew.

Finally, on Tuesday afternoon, the tests were fully completed, and the team of doctors stood around us both, impeccably dressed in their tailored suits and silk ties. "Mrs. Jackson, we find you to be in good health. You are free to schedule your flight back to Missouri."

"I think we'll go to Florida instead!" George said with a smile. I knew exactly what he meant: that everything we had worked so hard for could go forward just as we had always planned. It was late afternoon as we stepped through the lobby out into the fresh air. I was alive. I was thankful. But how do you live after believing you'll die? I couldn't understand what had just happened to me.

I looked back, the darkened figure in the stained glass paneling dulled by the bright rays of the Minnesota sun. It was St. Francis of Assisi—I recognized him now—and as I did, I remembered as a child learning his famous prayer about being an instrument of God's peace and love. Yet in the midst of my miracle I felt neither; I was still numb.

A bright yellow taxicab pulled up in front of the hospital. George opened the door. As I stepped in, the carillon bells rang from the Plummer tower downtown, chiming a celebratory rendition of Beethoven's *Ode to Joy*.

I hummed a few bars to myself before we sped away. I missed the rest.

Scan this code with your camera-equipped smartphone to view the companion video for Chapter Two. If you do not have the QR app on your phone, visit your app store and search for *QR code reader.*

THREE

MOON OVER MIAMI

You will show me the path of life.
Psalm 16:11

The water flowed up to my ankles and over my new sandals as I approached the phone booth. I didn't care. I didn't care that I was in the middle of a late afternoon downpour close to Miami. I didn't care, either, that I had just had an argument with George over a motel. There are some arguments in life that are simply worth having.

And this, without question, was one of them.

It had only been a few weeks since we had left Mayo Clinic. Doyle was just one month old, and we were reaching the end of our long, hot June journey to Florida. I felt like I had been holding my breath, riding an emotional roller-coaster of birth, death, hope, and despair, with three tired children in the backseat and an equally tired husband by my side.

And the motel that George pointed out from the

freeway was simply the last straw.

"It's a good option, Betty," he argued, wearily. "It will be fine until we get settled."

"It's probably the worst place for forty miles," I muttered under my breath, increasingly irritated. I wasn't going to spend the next few days staring at a concrete wall, being deafened by the noise of passing trucks.

"George!" I snapped. "I want a view of the beach and I want a pool."

"Betty, we're moving here for work," he shot back. "We're not on vacation!"

"George! I *need* a view of the beach." There was a startling fury in my tone, shocking even to me. "Stop the car and give me a dime!"

I held out my hand as George pulled over. His lips tightened, as though he were biting his tongue, and I caught Allen's eyes in the side mirror, glancing back and forth between the two of us. I knew what he was thinking and he was right: we were at it again. Florida was meant to give us a new start. No more veterinary school and no more conflict. Yet it seemed like we were picking up just where we had left off, before the nightmare in Missouri had begun.

Except this time, it was worse.

"May I *please* have a dime?" I said curtly, lowering my voice and slowing my words for dramatic effect. "I *would* like to choose the motel."

The subject was not open for discussion.

George relinquished with a sigh, and to his credit, he did so this time more quickly than usual. He didn't have the patience to go from place to place. He knew me better than to dig in deep and battle this one out. We were both tired, but it was pretty clear that I had more stamina for a fight.

I opened the car door and was drenched in an instant, before I even had time to slam it shut behind me. The rainwater was fresh and warm. I could taste the drops rolling down my face. The sidewalk was flooded, the phone booth too. Tiny eddies swirled round my feet as I stood there, my finger running through a dampened copy of the yellow pages.

My eyes scanned the columns of tightly printed text.

"That's it!" I cried out triumphantly. FAMILY RESORT, FORT LAUDERDALE BEACH. OCEAN VIEW. TV. SWIMMING POOL.

The dime dropped into the cash box with a faint clink, barely audible above the noise of the pounding torrent. I let out a sigh and promptly reserved the room without any hesitation. The price didn't really matter to me. I needed this.

As I stepped back toward the car, the rainstorm subsided almost as quickly as it had begun. I could feel the anger begin to drain from my face. I felt vindicated but empty, washed out and somewhat ashamed.

• • •

THE THREE BOYS WERE finally asleep. George opened the sliding glass door to the motel balcony and handed me a Styrofoam cup of coffee.

"Is it decaf?" I asked.

He nodded and, without thinking, started packing tobacco into his pipe. It was one of the briarwood pipes his grandfather had given him, and I knew he was quite attached to it. I watched out of the corner of my eye as he stood in the doorway and turned it round and round in his fingers. Was he going to light it? I wondered. Had he remembered our conversation in Columbia?

We had been packing up the house, getting ready to leave for Florida. Boxes were everywhere. George took a break, filled his pipe, and began to puff on it. Allen and Phillip took a sudden interest in what he was doing as smoke began to swirl in the air all around them. Doyle, who was nearby in a basket, started crying. "George," I said urgently, "we're going to have to live differently. We have three little boys now!" I had this strong feeling that we needed to change our lives somehow. George continued smoking, but from the way he looked at me, I knew I wasn't the only one evaluating our lives. He knew better than to smoke. When he was in embalming school, he had seen lungs black with cancer.

I took a sip of hot, steaming coffee while George

looked out over the ocean.

"It's nice, isn't it?"

I was quiet. The darkening blues of the eastern horizon met the ocean far off in the distance. There was hardly a cloud left in the sky and little evidence, if any, of the fierce storm that had caught us just a few hours earlier. But the storm clouds within took longer to dissipate. My emotions swirled and swelled inside my chest like the water in the phone booth.

"I have made a decision," George said resolutely.

I glanced at him.

"Betty, I'm putting the pipe away. I can't ask the boys to do something I'm not willing to do myself."

He put his pipe into his pocket and went back into the motel room, closing the sliding glass door behind him.

I turned my head away, back to the view. As I sat watching the waves, I saw a group of wading birds venture out to the water's edge. I had no idea what they were. They looked like tiny brown seagulls, their long spindly legs flocking to the freshly exposed stretches of sand left in the wake of the retreating tide. I could see them dipping their beaks, tirelessly, into hundreds of tiny air holes before rapidly flocking back as the water crept forward again.

I was grateful for the numbing motion, back and forth, back and forth. I closed my eyes and felt my breathing begin to slow, in and out, in and out, to the rhythm of the gently lapping foam . . .

But my mind was far from still. Scene by scene, the previous month's journey began to flash by: life with a newborn, the prospect of death, George's graduation, packing
up the house, saying goodbye to family and friends. Now,
here we were, at our destination, more than a thousand
miles from where we had begun. I felt unsettled and overwhelmed. I thought back to the car journey and, once
again, the ocean view. Finally my mind came to rest on a
poster I had seen in a filling station in southern Georgia.
Of all the moments I recalled, this random and seemingly
insignificant image preoccupied me the most. I had seen
the poster on a window at the gas station while we were
stretching our legs. It was a picture of Billy Graham, the
famous preacher. At the time he was still in his forties,
standing tall and confident in front of a crowd of thousands. In those days, the young Reverend Graham was
something of a celebrity. Everyone had heard of him, and
millions had responded to his simple call to faith. I myself
had never been to one of his crusades, but his voice echoed
around the nation and beyond. His distinctive North Car-
olinian accent would leap out from the radio as you tuned
through the frequencies. You couldn't escape it.

> *The ideals and ambitions you have now can*
> *make great men and women out of you.*
> *But you can't fulfill the promise of yourselves*
> *alone. You need Christ. You need Him right now.*

• • •

I COULDN'T MOVE. I had begun to feel a strange sensation as I stood in the hot sun; I felt my own weakness. Yet the longer I stared at this young preacher's face, the stronger I became, as though he was offering me the strength I was reaching for. I hesitated and heard his words again:

> *Without Him, you are in trouble.*
> *With Him, there can be no trouble too great*
> *for you to conquer. But you have to decide*
> *whether you will be with Him or without Him.*
> *The Bible says: "He who is not with me*
> *is against me." Where do you stand?*

I didn't really know what he meant. I wasn't against God. I had no problem with Him at all. I was just tired of church; something was missing for me. Besides, George was a good enough Christian for both of us. . . .

I opened my eyes and took a sip of cold coffee. The sun had long since set, and it was dark all around me. I stepped back into the bedroom. George had already fallen asleep.

• • •

THE BEACH VIEW LASTED less than a week. The boys and I would gladly have stayed longer, but we quickly arranged for us to settle into the North Miami neighborhood of Ives Dairy, in a comfortable tri-level house owned by a biology professor. The owner needed to take his family to Florida State University while he completed an advanced degree, and he was willing to rent his house out for a year. It was a nice home, perfect for our family: three or four miles from the beach, across the expressway. There were orange, lemon, and lime trees in the backyard. I was healthy and alive, and now that George was no longer studying, I was sure he would have more time to spend with the family.

At least that was the plan. The only problem was, once he began work, we didn't see much of George at all. His day began long before dawn when he would grab breakfast at the local diner by the racetracks. It ended, more often than not, well after dark, once the children were already asleep.

The first few weeks didn't bother me. I understood that he was laying a solid foundation for his ambition: to build a successful equine practice of his own.

George's mentor, Dr. M. B. Teigland, only twelve years his senior, was a handsome, mild-mannered man with blonde hair and kind eyes. With twenty years of experience behind him, he had established himself as one of the top equine specialists in the nation and was a frequent speaker at professional conferences. Dr. Teigland had a quick mind, an appreciation of the latest scientific advances, and a capacity for tireless work. Above all, he had an amiable, personal touch with the wealthy clientele that dominated the racetracks—the owners of horses valued at hundreds of thousands of dollars each.

George, as ever, was eager to learn. He had tremendous respect for Dr. Teigland and knew he needed to gain as much experience as possible. He wanted to specialize in the lameness of horses. This was not only a sought-after skill, but a superb opportunity for a young veterinarian. So, if it meant working long days, it was a price George was more than willing to pay. And I understood that for me, that was the cost of being married to a hard-working man.

But what I didn't understand was that horses, at that time, meant so much to George. He was eight when his grandfather had given him a pony for the summer months he spent at their home. From then on, they shared a horse together as long as his grandfather lived.

• • •

I DISTINCTLY REMEMBER the day George decided we needed to go back to church.

It was midsummer, and bright shafts of sunlight were beginning to stream in through the windows, carried from the east on the ocean breeze. I rolled over and sighed, my eyes adjusting to the light. I still couldn't get over the weather in Florida—it was perfect!

I glanced at the clock. George was up early. It couldn't be past seven yet. Soon, he walked into the room, dressed in his suit, adjusting a tie around his neck.

"We're going to church today," he said.

I winced at the thought. It wasn't so much that I was resisting it in principle—it was just that the last church we had attended had discouraged me so much. Our previous Sunday school teacher was dean of the nuclear physics department at the University of Missouri. He repeatedly told us there was no heaven or hell, no Daniel in the Lion's Den, no stone that killed Goliath. "The Bible isn't meant to be taken literally," he would say. But it never made any sense to me. If Christianity was built on myths and allegories, then why bother with it at all?

Once in a while, I would ask George, "George, if there's really no heaven or hell, why don't we just stay home and read the newspapers and drink coffee? Polishing the boys' little white shoes takes a lot of time and work!"

I watched George's reflection in the mirror as he pulled his tie loose and started over again. "I hope this church is different from the one we attended in Columbia," I said.

"Well, we should still go to church on Sunday," George stated matter-of-factly.

"I know, George," I said, frustrated. "That's not the

point. Everyone goes to church on Sunday. I just hope we find someplace more meaningful!"

"We're going to Hollywood Hills Methodist, and we're going as a family," George declared.

I tried to go back to sleep but couldn't. Doyle stirred in his crib. My raised voice had disturbed him.

● ● ●

SO, THAT'S HOW WE ENDED UP in Hollywood Hills that Sunday morning. George was a stickler about going to the Methodist church, and this one was only five miles from our house: the trip took about twelve minutes along the back roads that ran parallel to the expressway. It was a modern, sand-colored sanctuary with a wide sloping roof, surrounded by an expanse of neatly mown grass. The neighborhood was pleasant enough too: bigger lots, palm trees, and swimming pools.

It was 9:15 a.m. The boys were fed, neatly dressed, and we had made it in good time. We were greeted at the glass-fronted portico by a young, well-dressed woman who introduced herself as Velma Frank.

"It's good to see you," she said in a sincere and friendly voice. "Is this your first time here?" I nodded nervously and explained we had just moved to the area.

"I'll help you get the children settled into their Sunday school classes. Then why don't you come upstairs and join ours? My husband is leading the class today; I think you'll enjoy it."

"Of course," I replied, warming to her. "We would love to."

The room was brightly lit, with ten or twelve rows of grey metal chairs. I nervously looked at George and then glanced around. There were twenty or twenty-five married couples. All were educated professionals, by the looks of it, starting out, like us, with new families and careers.

A tall, well-spoken man in his early thirties stood up with a broad, welcoming smile. "Hi! I'm Neil Frank," he began warmly. "I'm president of the young couples Sunday school class here at Hollywood Hills Methodist. I work at the National Hurricane Center in Miami. I think most of you know my beautiful wife, Velma." She blushed.

"Our new teacher, Bud Cobb, couldn't be here to-day," he continued, "so I'll be filling in for him. I see a few new people, so please, introduce yourselves—there are no strangers here."

We went around the room, each saying a few words. I couldn't possibly remember all the names, but there were a few that stood out. Bob Feller was the first to speak. He was a radio announcer who had recently moved with his wife, Nadine, from Rockford, Illinois—they were Midwesterners like us. Next to them sat a vibrant, good-natured woman named Sherry Taylor. She had a quick wit and a soft Georgian drawl that made me feel instantly at ease. Her husband, Bob, was a former FSU football player who now worked as a salesman, attending conventions in upscale Miami hotels on behalf of the tobacco company Liggett & Myers. Across the aisle sat Marie, a quiet, tall, dark-haired woman, with her husband, C. B. She was serious and thoughtful, working on a PhD in education, and she played an important role in the Dade County school system. To her right sat her antithesis, Sharon, an artistic girl with long hair, beads, and a flower-patterned dress, the wife of a mortician. The pastor's daughter Anne, an attractive redhead, listened behind them on the back row, where she was seated next to her husband, an attorney. She seemed a little detached from the others.

The gilt edges of Neil's new Bible caught my attention. He was flipping through the pages, trying to find his place.

"As most of you know," Neil said, "Bud's received permission to change our curriculum. We're no longer using the Methodist Quarterly."

"It's a real shame too," quipped Sherry from the front. "Poor Neil doesn't have half as much time to talk about the weather anymore!"

A ripple of laughter darted across the room—everyone appeared to be quite comfortable with each other. "Instead," he emphasized, "we're studying the Gospel of Mark. Let's pick up where we left off in Mark, chapter four."

"Betty, we were meant to bring a Bible." George whispered in my ear. He was always so anxious to do the right thing.

Neil continued reading,

> *Listen! A farmer went to sow his seed. As he was scattering the seed, some fell along the path, and the birds came and ate it up. Some fell on rocky places, where it did not have much soil. It sprang up quickly, because the soil was shallow. But when the sun came up, the plants were scorched, and they withered because they had no root. Other seed fell among thorns, which grew up and choked the plants, so that they did not bear grain. Still other seed fell on good soil. It came up, grew and produced a crop, some multiplying thirty, some sixty, some a hundred times.*
> Mark 4:3-8 (NIV)

"So, folks," Neil interjected enthusiastically, "what does this make you think about?"

"My *flowers*," Sherry joked again, "they are wilting in this heat!"

"I always thought it was about how people approach the Bible," piped up Bob Feller.

"Isn't it more about your attitude toward God?" suggested Marie.

"I was thinking the same thing," said Neil. "I was driving down I-95 this week, wondering about my own attitude toward God. Ever since Bud challenged us to read the Bible, I have been doing so every day. And this week, I came across a phrase that shocked me: that sin is anything I do that falls short of God's will. I never thought I was a sinner before, but the Bible tells me that I am!"

I stared at this good-looking, educated man in disbelief. He had just called himself a sinner.

Neil continued, "I found myself praying, 'If there is a God up there somewhere and I'm a sinner, then *I* need a Savior.'"

"What a relief," I thought excitedly to myself. "This seems to be real to them!" And to my surprise, I found myself standing up in the middle of the class.

"It is so *good* to be in a church where they are actually studying the Bible!" I exclaimed. Something deep within me was responding and I couldn't understand why. I looked around the room at the faces, feeling encouraged. "Thank you so much. I'm so happy to be here." I felt my eyes fill with tears.

A chair creaked as someone stood up behind me. It was Anne, the pastor's daughter.

"Oh, don't worry, honey," she said in a patronizing tone. "We don't *really* believe it!"

No one else spoke up, and I quietly sat down, completely deflated. For the rest of the class, and in the worship service that followed, I didn't say or hear another word. Church was going progressively downhill for me.

On the way out of church, Velma stopped us again.

"May I have your phone number?" she said without hesitation. "And please let me know if there is any way we can help you get settled." I quickly gave her our number.

George walked ahead and unlocked the car as the older boys climbed in. I felt strong disappointment.

"George, I am *never* going back to another Methodist Sunday school. I want to go help with the children downstairs instead."

"Oh, come on, Betty, it wasn't that bad. I liked what they had to say," said George.

"I'm not going back," I said firmly. "If they don't believe it, then why should I?"

• • •

LUNCH WAS BARELY FINISHED when the phone began to ring. We normally managed to get through the Sunday roast without interruption, but in recent weeks, the calls had started coming earlier and earlier. There was always a horse that needed attention and, as the most junior member of the practice, George had to field most of the calls himself.

"I shouldn't be long," he said cheerfully, as he turned to go out to his station wagon. I didn't say anything. It was unlikely he would be home before dark.

It was after dinner, and I had just finished the evening baths.

"Let's go for a bike ride," I announced.

"But, where's Daddy?" said Phillip, puzzled.

"He's with the horses, and he won't be back till late. Come on, boys, get your shoes."

I placed Doyle in the basket and Phillip on the frame, between the seat and the handlebars, while I climbed up right behind him. Allen sat on the carrier over the rear wheel. Then we set off through the neighborhood, just like that, while we watched the moon come up over the skyline of Miami.

It felt like I was running away, but I had no idea from what. Just a few short weeks ago, I would have done anything to know I had this life ahead of me, but now I found myself more miserable than ever. It wasn't the cancer or the move or the pressure of looking after three small children. It wasn't even the loneliness or the fact that George was so busy at work. I knew I could cope with any of these, if only the ache inside would just go away. But it wouldn't because, frankly, it had started long before. Long before any diagnosis, long before Doyle, perhaps even before Phillip and Allen.

The bicycle coasted down an incline, and I felt the evening breeze blow my hair behind me. I could hear Phillip's squeals and feel Allen's tightening grip round my waist. A full moon was rising in the twilight ahead. I loved it: the weightlessness, the freedom, the view . . .

If only I could make it last.

Back home, the ache got steadily worse. George phoned, apologetically, to let me know he was on his way. The older boys had already gone to bed. Only Doyle was awake, playing in his crib, getting ready for one last bottle. I remembered back to when Allen was first born, how he would lie on his back in that same crib in our house in Kansas City, and Phillip, when his turn came, in our house in Columbia. When did this ache start? Had it been there all along?

The phone rang again. Startled, I rushed to the kitchen to get it.

But instead of George, it was Velma Frank from the church. At first, I was surprised; I didn't expect her to call me so soon. Just as she started talking, I heard Doyle's faint cries as he lay in his crib. I stretched the telephone cord as far as it would go, one hand holding the receiver, the other reaching around the corner to Doyle. I stood there for some time, stroking him gently on the back, while Velma made small talk, telling me a little bit more about herself. Finally, Doyle settled. I slipped off my sandals, then slid down the doorway to the floor, stretching my legs out in front of me.

"What about you?" Velma asked.

The house was quiet and my thoughts so persistent

that I found myself beginning to pour them all out: the experience at Mayo Clinic, the move from Missouri, the feelings of numbness, and the sense of despair.

"My dear," her soft voice interrupted, "there's a lady in the Sunday school class who lives in your neighborhood. Would you mind if I give her your number?"

• • •

THE NEXT MORNING, Sherry called. I recognized her accent immediately.

"Betty Jackson," she began, without any introduction, "Velma told me she thought you needed a friend."

"Well we're new here—" I began to explain.

"Now, I'm not a very good one," Sherry continued, cutting me off playfully, "but I live round the corner and I'll happily fill in while you're looking for one. May I stop by for coffee?"

I couldn't help laughing as we talked for a while. There was something very disarming about her, and we actually had much in common. She also stayed home with two small children, and we quickly became close, like sisters. But though the relationship with Sherry certainly eased the loneliness, it did little to relieve the emptiness I felt.

"I think you should try the Sunday school class again," George announced one night at the dinner table. He was home uncharacteristically early, and I guess he thought that gave him a right to try pushing, once more, on that firmly locked door. "You never did meet Bud, the teacher of the class. He's a wonderful man: an airline pilot. And he's teaching us the Bible. I'm learning a lot. You should come back too."

"I don't care, George!" I snapped. "He can teach it all he likes, but if he doesn't believe it, why should I?"

"An airline pilot," said Phillip, "flying airplanes!"

"But he does, Betty," George argued. "He does believe it, that's my point!"

"Mommy, I want to ride in a plane!" demanded Phillip.

"Be quiet," Allen elbowed Phillip.

"Listen," I said, my voice rising. "We have been to church all our lives, but we both know something is missing. If I died, I would go straight to hell, I know I would, George! Being a Methodist won't save me, and I'm not even sure it will save you!"

There was a moment's silence. Phillip was looking down at his food, but Allen's worried eyes were fixed on mine. It was a look that tore my heart. Regardless, I turned my head away and carried on. I had started now and I wasn't going to stop. "I just don't want to go anymore!"

I picked up the dinner plates, stacking them unnecessarily high, and headed to the kitchen sink.

"What's your problem?"

I whirled back around, shocked to the core, and found myself staring speechless at George.

"My *problem?* Nothing! I'm happy, downstairs, with the children. That's all!"

"Mommy, you don't look very happy," Allen said softly beneath his breath. The plates crashed into the sink and I walked out of the room. He was right, I wasn't. I just didn't know why. And it wouldn't go away . . .

As a child, I heard the Bible stories, I heard my parents pray, I knew God was real, but I turned away. I became rebellious toward God.

Scan this code with your camera-equipped smartphone to view the companion video for Chapter Three. If you do not have the QR app on your phone, visit your app store and search for *QR code reader*.

FOUR

LET ME KNOW THE TRUTH

Jesus answered,
"I am the way and the truth and the life."
John 14:6 (NIV)

Then Jesus caught me by surprise.

It was fall in Florida—five months since the move. The tropical afternoon rainstorms were gone, as well as the stifling humidity of summer. Our first hurricane season was also over, including the curious drama of watching George balance on a stepladder, trimming the ficus trees in the front yard as the Atlantic gales drew near.

Thanksgiving was around the corner. We had settled in well. We had even made some good friends at the Methodist church in Hollywood Hills, in spite of my vow not to go back to Sunday school.

But why did I feel so different? That pervading sense of emptiness remained, stubborn and irrational as ever. It was maybe pushed down a little deeper below the surface by the constant activity of the boys, the household chores, and the daily routine.

Indeed, my life was a gift. But I kept wondering what I should do with it!

Surprisingly enough, I found myself singing Bible songs with Phillip and the rest of the preschoolers at church and actually enjoying them. We would listen to the lesson and then act out the chorus together:

> *The wise man built his house upon the rock,*
> *The wise man built his house upon the rock,*
> *The wise man built his house upon the rock,*
> *And the rain came tumbling down . . .*

Each week, as "the rain came down and the floods rose up," the peals of laughter would reach a crescendo as all the toddlers went crashing to the floor, just like the foolish man's house that was built on sand. But then, when the singing was over, I would find myself standing outside George's Sunday school class, trying my best to keep Doyle and Phillip at peace.

One Sunday, Velma and Sherry were the first to come out, heading quickly to the nursery to pick up their children.

"Sorry we went on a bit, Betty. Time just flies in there!" said Velma as she rushed by.

"Man! I thought that would never end," Sherry said with a grin. "You missed a good lesson today. You should join us, sometime, Betty."

"It's not for me," I replied politely; but I was a little intrigued all the same. I was sure that I didn't want to go back to the class: I couldn't face being disappointed again. But at the same time, I had a strange feeling that I was missing out on something.

"Where did you get that outfit?" I quickly asked Sherry, changing the subject. "That color looks really nice on you." We started to walk down the hall together.

"You're only saying that because it would look good on you," she teased. She was right: our friends joked about us looking and acting like twins.

"Betty Joyce!" George's voice carried down the corridor. I turned around. "What?" I asked. George was obviously quite excited about something.

"Bud's invited us over to his house after church." He took one look at my face, then quickly added, "His wife, Dot, will be there too," hoping that her name would somehow tip the balance in his favor.

I thought for a minute. "Well, I guess we can go," I replied reluctantly, "but not for long. Lunch is in the oven."

"Dad, Dad! May I go with you this afternoon?" Allen pleaded, staring up at both of us with his hopeful brown eyes as we walked out into the sunshine toward the car. He loved to ride in the station wagon when George went to visit the country farms; he would help carry a pail of water or some medication—maybe even hold the halter of one of the horses. It was a big deal for an eight-year-old, and he always returned full of stories.

"I want to go too!" chimed in Phillip.

"Dad!" Allen quietly protested.

"Allen, you may come." There was instant silence. George was respected by the boys and they had learned not to talk back. "Now climb in," he said, firmly, as he held their door open and waited for everyone to get settled. As he started the car and pulled out of the parking lot, I glanced at my watch.

"We can stay for fifteen minutes at the most, George," I reminded him.

His lips closed tightly, but he kept quiet and nodded. I looked out the window, an uneasy feeling in the pit of my stomach. It was kind of Bud and Dot to invite us over, but there seemed to be more to this invitation than a courtesy call.

"This looks like a nice neighborhood," I observed after several minutes of silence. I loved the sprawling Florida homes. Built on one level, so as to have a better chance of withstanding the hurricanes, they looked so elegant, surrounded by symmetrically placed palms and bushes and bright tropical flowers. The street sign caught my eye as George began to slow down and turn onto Jackson Street.

"Is this it?" I asked, admiring their beautiful home.

George didn't reply. Instead, he stopped the car, turned around in his seat and started giving instructions to the boys.

"Allen, you're in charge. Mother and I won't be long," he said. "Roll down the windows. Give Doyle some air. Take him out of his infant seat if he wakes up."

Phillip immediately responded by rolling his window up and down. Allen frowned, clearly not too thrilled with his newfound responsibilities.

As we walked toward the house, Bud was already at the front door with a welcoming smile. He appeared to be a few years older than us, in his late thirties, and I immediately noticed his twinkling eyes.

"Hi, George! Betty, I'm Bud," he said, reaching over to shake my hand, "and this is my wife, Dot," he added. She stood a few steps behind him, noticeably taller, an elegant woman with straight brown hair.

"Good timing, George," she said graciously. "We just got home."

"What a lovely home!" I said, looking around the spacious living room. It was tastefully decorated, and through the kitchen I could see patio doors opening onto a pool.

"Lemonade for you both?" offered Dot, heading into the kitchen. We nodded.

"May I help at all?" I asked, touched by their genuine warmth.

"No, no. Please sit down. I'll be right back," she said, pointing to the couch. "Please!"

We sat next to each other and I looked up at George.

"What next?" I thought. There was a moment's silence as Bud cleared his throat.

"Betty," he began, slowly and deliberately. "I have gotten to know George a little bit in the Sunday school class." He cocked his head to one side and smiled. There was something quite compelling about him—his obvious love of life and enthusiasm for people. I found myself beginning to relax.

"The class doesn't always give us an opportunity to talk one on one. Yet I have noticed George has a real interest in what we have been studying. I would call it a hunger," he continued, tilting his head once again as he smiled.

I glanced at George. It was true. He often talked about Bud and the class, and even now he appeared to be hanging on his every word. He did look hungry. In fact, it was the first time I had seen him this absorbed in something other than his horses.

"If it's okay with you," Bud continued gently as Dot entered with a tray of cookies and lemonade, "I wanted to tell you both my story."

George looked at his watch, and then at me.

"The boys are waiting in the car," he explained, "but we have a few minutes."

"I'm a pilot," Bud said proudly, diving right in. "I have loved airplanes ever since I was four years old and saw pictures of the first flight to New York taking off from Pan American Field. As a little guy, they grabbed me." He snapped his fingers, eyes wide open for effect.

"So at the end of World War II, I volunteered for the Air Force and spent two years learning all they would teach me. When I got out, I went to work at the new airport in Miami. I did every job I could, earning five dollars a day— enough to get my commercial license.

"I got my first pilot's job, based out of Jacksonville, in 1951. Then, out of the blue, my dad came down with an aneurism of the heart. His blood was pumping five times faster than it should have. So I went to the doctor, looked him in the eyes and said, 'Tell me the truth, how long does he have?'

"The doctor hesitated. 'A man in his condition might live two weeks at the most,' he told me.

"'Two weeks!'" Bud paused and looked up, catching my eye.

"I left the hospital and, right there in my truck, I prayed: 'Lord, I don't think my dad is ready to stand before you. If you spare him, I'll do my best to prepare him. I'll do my best to tell him the truth!'"

George glanced across at me, trying to gauge my reaction. Even if my lips were silent, my face was an open book. I knew exactly what Bud was talking about. The desperation I had felt on the way to Mayo Clinic had not yet left me.

"Anyways," Bud continued, "I was sitting there praying for my dad when God's peace suddenly flooded me from head to toe. He had heard my prayer and I knew it. Right away, Dot and I knew there was something more to being a Christian than just attending church."

Bud's glass of lemonade stood there untouched, sweated beads of water forming a small puddle on the clear glass coffee table. There was a strange sense of urgency to the moment.

"Meanwhile, the pastor of our Methodist church asked me to teach Sunday school, and in order to teach, I had to prepare. So I decided I should start reading the Bible—to figure out what I believed."

"What *do* you believe?" asked George.

Bud leaned forward slowly, hands clasped together. "As a pilot," he replied, looking straight at us, "I have to know two things: Where am I now? And where am I going? I discovered something," he said earnestly, pointing with his index finger. "We are lost in a wilderness. There is no way out on our own. Jesus is the Way. And if we want Him to lead us, He can't just be our Savior—he has to be our Lord."

He could see us both staring at him, somewhat confused.

"I was in a hotel room, between flights, when it finally hit me. I had to receive Jesus as Savior *and* Lord. It wasn't good enough just to believe He existed—somewhere up there." Bud looked up toward the ceiling and then shut his eyes, as if in prayer. "I told God: 'I want you to be my

Lord.' And bit by bit, I started to surrender everything: my car, my bank account, my wife, my children . . .

"'Keep going,' I heard God say, as plain as day."

George and I just stared at him in silence. My heart was beating faster. I put my hand over my chest as if to quiet it. How could he have heard God talking to *him?* I wondered, studying his face. I had never heard anyone tell a story like this!

"I asked God, 'Isn't that *enough?*'" Bud's narrative was gathering momentum as he acted out his argument.

"But it wasn't! Then I was bombarded and taunted by a different voice in my head: 'Do you understand what you are doing? This is gonna be it for you. Try and have a life after this un-con-di-tion-al surrender.' It struck me then," Bud declared solemnly, "that I couldn't surrender flying. It was my lifelong ambition. I just couldn't do it. I couldn't possibly give it up. I rubbed my arms at the mere thought. Sitting in that hotel room, I broke out in a cold sweat. I wrestled with that thought for nearly an hour. Finally I gave in. I felt His presence fill me and envelop me as never before.

"I went back to teach the Sunday school and God's Spirit moved. They started receiving Jesus into their hearts, including my dad. He lived another six years after that!" Bud paused.

Suddenly the story was over, and Bud fixed his gaze directly on us. "George and Betty, has anyone ever told you how you can be saved? How you can know Jesus as your personal Savior?"

We both shook our heads. "No."

"Would you like me to?"

"Yes," said George, with such speed and urgency that it took me by surprise. He set his drink down with a clink and knelt beside the coffee table. "What do I do?"

"It's simple," Bud replied. "I'm going to say a prayer with you, and you can repeat it after me." He then turned and looked at me. There was an embarrassing silence. My heart began to beat even faster. This was *my* opportunity. I slipped off the couch and onto my knees beside George.

"Heavenly Father," Bud began, with George and me echoing in reply: "I kneel before you today as a sinner that needs a Savior. I believe you sent Jesus to the Cross to die for my sins. He took my punishment so I can be free. Forgive me and change me. Come into my heart by the power of your Spirit. I ask you, Lord Jesus, to be my Savior and my Lord—from this day forward and for the rest of my life. Amen."

Phrase by phrase, we repeated his words. Even Dot joined in, quietly, from the armchair across the room. It was simple and ordinary. We just knelt at the coffee table and said a prayer, that's all. Nothing dramatic happened, no lightning strikes, no voices from heaven. I glanced at George and he looked the same. I suppose I did too. We stood up. Fifteen minutes had passed. The boys had probably had enough by now.

George shook Bud's hand. "Thank you for your time. I'll see you next week."

"Thanks for the lemonade," I told Dot, and followed George out the door.

● ● ●

"MOTHER, WHAT TOOK YOU SO LONG?" Phillip asked, his face flushed from the heat, as he peered out of the open car window. George had stopped on the sidewalk, looking at the children but somehow staring past them.

"We accepted Jesus in our hearts," I said simply.

"Can we go now, Dad?" said Allen quietly.

George calmly stepped into the car, turned the key in the ignition, and started to drive. The refreshing air blew through the open windows, and I pulled my hair back into a short ponytail, trying to grasp what had just happened.

"Do you remember that camp experience I told you about?" George asked unexpectedly.

I nodded my head. George had talked about it a few times.

It was the summer before we started dating. He was fifteen at the time and went to a Church camp in Fayetteville, Arkansas, not far from the foothills of the Ozark Mountains. That Friday night there was a guest speaker. George heard him issue a challenge to "give all you have!"

George, who sitting near the back, made his way to the front of the room, knelt down, and emptied his pockets of all the money he had. He was sure he wanted to make a commitment, but he didn't know how to respond. There was no one to help him.

The following Sunday, the pastor called the youth who had responded at the camp up to the front of the church, where the congregation filed by and shook their hands. "Why in the world are they shaking my hand?" George wondered. "What did *I* do?!"

"Now I finally understand," George explained. "I felt God moving in my life, and I needed to respond; to ask Jesus into my life. Betty, it's as though I have been at that camp altar for fourteen years, waiting for someone to lead me to salvation!"

His voice faltered. "You know, you can spend your whole life in church and never meet God." George held the steering wheel tight with both hands, his speech fraying into fragments of emotion. I was astounded; I had never seen George cry. He didn't often display a lot of emotion.

"All your life, you have lived aware you were a sinner and enjoyed it," he said, looking straight at me. "I have lived as a sinner and been miserable!"

There was George's straightforwardness for you. He was right: I *had* lived as a sinner and I hadn't exactly been miserable. That was the truth! At least, not until the last six months.

• • •

I CAN'T SAY that George and I changed much over the following days, but our choices did. We had a desire to read our Bibles, something that neither of us had ever done before, at least not on our own. First, we found ourselves in the bookstore, buying two "Amplified" New Testaments. Then we started to read them for ourselves. Three nights in a row, George came back early from the racetracks and we spent the evenings reading together.

"Look, Betty," he would say, "Jesus says that the pure in heart will see God. Can you imagine actually seeing God? Wouldn't you like to?"

"I would be happy just to hear him," I would reply. "I'm still not sure that he really speaks to people like he did to Bud. But if He does, I want him to speak to me."

Then it would be my turn. "George, Jesus says in John 10:27 'My sheep listen to my voice. I know them and they follow me.'"

Less than a week had passed since we knelt together by the glass-topped coffee table in the Cobbs' living room. There was a part of me that was beginning to wonder whether we had just gotten caught up in the enthusiasm of the moment and whether that prayer had really changed anything at all.

Still, I was enjoying this newfound sense of purpose. George seemed more attentive, more engaged—and finally he had let me in on a passion of his that I could truly share.

It was a Thursday. I had just given Doyle and Phillip their lunch and was in the kitchen cleaning the countertops when I heard a clear voice above me.

I heard these words: "You said . . ."

I looked up, startled.

Doyle was lying on a blanket in the middle of the floor, contentedly kicking his feet, and Phillip was riding his push car round and round on the patio, just outside the kitchen door.

"You said, 'let me know the truth before I die.'"

Dishcloth in hand, I looked up at the ceiling in astonishment. I was hearing an audible voice, but I was alone. No one else was in the house!

Suddenly, my mind flashed back to my journey to Mayo Clinic; I had all but forgotten that one desperate prayer: "God, please let me know the truth, before I die, so I can tell it to my children."

"Yes, I did say that."

"I am the Truth!"

I had heard that phrase somewhere before. I ran to the bedroom to get my Bible and brought it back to the kitchen table. As I put it down, the pages fell open at John, chapter fourteen. My eyes scanned down the page and stopped at verse six.

Jesus answered, "I am the way and
the truth and the life. No one comes to the
Father except through me." (NIV1984)

At that moment, everything changed. The Bible was
not just real, it was alive! There was a God—He was real—
and He was speaking to me! For the first time in my life, I
had found the Truth.

Hungrily, I read on.

If you really knew me, you would know
my Father as well. From now on, you
do know him and have seen him. (NIV1984)

I knew, then, that the truth was not whether I was
a Baptist, a Methodist, a Catholic or a Jew. But it was
whether I knew Jesus.

Jesus, Himself, was the Truth.

Doyle was still on his blanket. Phillip was still careening
around outside. But everything in my life had instantly
changed.

Grace and truth came through Jesus Christ.

Tears were falling from my eyes even before my head
sank to the table and I started sobbing, finally able to
release the numbness, the despair, and the fear I had felt
for months. In rushed the joy: I could feel life coming into
me and healing me. So many things started to make sense:

my diagnosis, the desperation, and the journey to Mayo Clinic. It wasn't just luck or a doctor's mistake. Jesus had healed me so I could teach the truth to my children.

"Phillip, come here!"

Phillip stood at the patio door, took one look at me, and rushed into the kitchen, his eyes wide in alarm. "Mommy, what's wrong with you?"

"I'm so happy!" I said, tears running down my cheeks. "I'm so happy!" I had never felt such joy and peace. "I'm happy!" and I burst out laughing. That was the truth!

I scooped Doyle up in one arm, grabbed Phillip's hand, and started dancing around the room. Their giggles and laughter soon joined with mine until we collapsed on the floor in a big pile, completely out of breath.

"Mommy, let's do it again!" Phillip shouted.

I was still laughing as I explained. "Phillip, do you know what just happened to Mommy?" I grabbed my Bible off the table, "Jesus just spoke to me and told me He was the Way, the Truth, and the Life. Phillip, do you understand what that means?" He looked up at me quizzically.

I read to him from John 14.

> *And I will ask the Father, and he will give you another Counselor to be with you forever—the Spirit of truth… Before long, the world will not see me anymore, but you will see me… Because I live, you also will live.* (NIV1984)

I looked up at the calendar on the wall. It was November 1965—six months since I first entered the hospital in Columbia. Then it hit me: my six months were up and I was still alive.

The life I was living was no longer my own.

Scan this code with your camera-equipped smartphone to view the companion video for Chapter Four. If you do not have the QR app on your phone, visit your app store and search for *QR code reader.*

FIVE

Speaking in Spanish

You will be my witnesses...
to the ends of the earth.
Acts 1:8 (NIV)

The exhilaration lasted for more than three days. I remember hanging up the clothes to dry in the backyard, one minute crying, the next laughing, as I lifted the damp shirts from the basket and fastened them tightly to the outstretched line. I was beginning to wonder what the neighbors must be thinking, but the truth was, I couldn't stop thinking about them.

"What if *they* don't know Jesus?" I would say to myself as I peered across the narrow lawns that separated our homes. And, every time I did, I would feel a weight pressing down on my chest. I began to look for ways to get to know them. I knew I couldn't keep what I had learned to myself for very long!

The Kassenheimers were a large Catholic family with eight children who lived a few doors down. Our boys loved playing together. Often, at dinnertime, I ended up standing on their doorstep talking to their mother when I went to call Allen and Phillip home.

"May I share something with you?" I ventured one day, surprising even myself.

"Of course, Betty," she replied kindly.

"About six months ago, I was diagnosed with breast cancer. I was told I was dying and I didn't know where I would spend eternity."

Mrs. Kassenheimer's eyes winced with concern.

"I found myself praying a simple prayer, asking God to show me the truth before I died so I could teach it to my children. A few days later, I was cancer-free. For the longest time, I didn't understand, but now I know it was Jesus who healed me. It's knowing Him as your Savior that matters, not where you go to church."

A few days later, she sent me a thank you note and a large batch of oatmeal raisin cookies, enough for a family double our size. Encouraged, I looked for more opportunities, wherever they might come.

And they came, one by one.

"Hi, I'm Betty," I said, as I handed a package to the lady who lived next door. "I think the postman delivered this to us by mistake."

The lady thanked me and was about to go back inside, when I found myself seizing the moment to tell my story. "You know," I began, "just six months ago, I was dying of cancer." Her eyes narrowed skeptically as she listened. "But Jesus healed me," I continued, "and a few weeks ago I met Him as my Savior."

"I'm not interested," she answered curtly. "I'm a Jehovah's Witness." And with that, she shut the door in my face.

I stood there, disheartened, realizing that my neighborhood mission might require a little more prayer. So from that night on, after reading a Bible story to the boys, we would gather together to pray.

"We ask that our friends and our neighbors would meet Jesus like we have. Amen."

Over the next few weeks, I walked up and down the street, visiting homes in Ives Dairy, feeling an urgency to share about Jesus with everyone I met. The reactions were mixed, but my fervor was undiminished—I was so glad to be saved. And one night, just as I was getting ready to serve dinner, Phillip rushed triumphantly through the front door.

"Allen, Allen, come see what I have!" he said proudly as he poured out a brown paper bag of candy onto the living room floor, jaw breakers and tootsie pops scattering everywhere. "I just went trick or treating!" he declared, his four-year-old eyes twinkling with excitement. "I knocked on doors, just like Mommy!"

• • •

IT WAS TRUE that I had promised myself that I would never go back to Sunday school, but a new Monday night Bible study had just started at Bud's house. They were getting together to read through the New Testament. There was only one rule: you could ask any question you wanted, but first, you had to look through the Bible, *yourself,* for the answer.

The next Monday evening, George made a point of coming home early. We left the boys with a babysitter and set off on the short, five-mile drive toward Hollywood Hills. There were quite a few people we recognized instantly: Neal, Velma, Sherry, Marie, the Fellers, and several others. We soon learned that George and I weren't the only ones who had knelt at Bud's coffee table and prayed! Everyone, it seemed, had a similar story.

"I met Jesus at the kitchen sink," I began, without hesitation. "He spoke four simple words to me: 'I am the Truth!'"

"That's amazing," interjected Velma. "Last week He said something similar to me! I saw the room fill with light and I felt God's presence all around me. Then I heard this still, small voice deep within say: 'I am the Light of the world!'"

"I've been searching for something," George admitted when his turn came, his eyes moist with emotion, "ever since I was fifteen. I didn't know how to find it. But now I have found *Him.*"

Nadine Feller spoke up next.

"I was raised in a Christian home, and when I was sitting in church one day, my older brother told me that if I didn't put up my hand, I would go to hell." Everyone laughed. "But I never really understood what that meant until now."

She wasn't alone. There was something remarkable taking place in this unlikely group of young married couples. Most of us had been churchgoers all our lives, but like Nadine, we had never understood what it meant to encounter Christ for ourselves. Nor was this wave of the Holy Spirit limited to our Bible study. There were half a dozen similar home groups starting up in our area, and hundreds more across the United States. We were part of a movement that was spreading across the world. Denominational barriers that had held firm for generations were beginning to break down. God was sovereignly revealing Himself to ordinary people: to me in the kitchen as 'the Way, the Truth and the Life,' to Velma in Bud's living room as the 'Light of the world.'

And that light was spreading.

George and I thought nothing of driving for an hour or two in the evening to hear one of the many visiting Bible teachers who would crisscross the nation, ministering in various churches, hotel ballrooms, or homes. Occasionally, they would come and speak in Bud's living room on a Monday night, or at one of the local monthly meetings organized by the Full Gospel Businessmen's Fellowship in Miami, Fort Lauderdale, or as far north as West Palm Beach.

• • •

"PLEASE MOVE toward the center of your row," said the confident-looking businessman at the front of the hall. He was dressed in a navy blue sports jacket and neatly pressed grey slacks, and he certainly didn't look like one of those half-crazed "holy rollers" I'd always heard tales about. "Let's make room for those who are still arriving." The grand ballroom of the Sheraton Beach Hotel could hold more than four hundred people, but there must have been far more of us crammed into the aisles and doorways that night. It was January in Fort Lauderdale, and the city's population had swelled with the "snow birds" from the north. A profound sense of anticipation hung in the air.

"Tonight we're going to hear three testimonies," said our host, quieting the room. "We have invited three men from very different professions to share how their lives have been impacted by the power of the Holy Spirit: a federal court judge, a television entrepreneur, and an Episcopal priest!"

The first to take the podium was Judge Kermit Bradford from Atlanta, a distinguished man in his late fifties. His story was riveting. As a young criminal defense attorney, he agreed to prove the innocence of a murderer held on death row. And, in the process, they both gave their lives to Jesus.

After him, a young man named Pat Robertson took the stage. Only thirty-five years old, he had already served in Korea, graduated with a law degree from Yale, and been to seminary. But after encountering the Holy Spirit while praying at his sick son's bedside, he had felt the call of God to establish the nation's first Christian television network. "I remember picking up a book in the library by the great nineteenth-century evangelist Charles Finney," Pat began, his imposing frame towering over the lectern. "I, like Finney, had started out as a lawyer, so I took the book home to read. I was astonished at what I found. Finney claimed to have been baptized in the Holy Spirit and to have spoken in other tongues, just like the disciples in Acts, chapter two. "Once I had read it, I could hardly sleep," he continued, while all around us, the ballroom stilled to a hush. "Finney attributed his experience to nothing more than a reckless quest for God. So I decided, with a few close friends, to take three days off and find a quiet place where we could fast and pray. We ended up, by chance, in an abandoned farmhouse deep in the woods of Connecticut. There, down a small path in the brush, we came across a clearing. In the middle of it stood a simple stone monument:

BIRTHPLACE OF CHARLES G. FINNEY 1792

ATTORNEY, EVANGELIST, COLLEGE PRESIDENT, MAN OF GOD.

"It was as though we were on holy ground and God was about to pour Himself out on us, even as He did on Finney."

I looked up at George, then down the row of chairs at our friends from the Monday night Bible study, who flanked us on either side. Everyone around me seemed to be caught up in the excitement and anticipation of the moment; George even more so than the others. But I was nervous. As a child, the church we attended did not teach about speaking in tongues. I don't even remember hearing it mentioned.

Yet I couldn't deny the uncompromising challenge of this young man's faith and the humility with which he shared his journey. He had heard the call of God, defied his rich and powerful father, and, together with his wife, given up everything—even their wedding gifts—so he could go to Bible school in New York. They moved to an undesirable area of the city, ate soy beans, and started a family. And when they arrived in Virginia in 1959, he set out to buy a bankrupt television station with only seventy dollars in his pocket.

After Pat Robertson sat down, there was a brief intermission. George was visibly stirred. He shuffled his feet anxiously on the carpet, impatient to hear more. His notebook was filled with writing. At the top, underlined several times, was the phrase "reckless quest," beneath it, "Acts, chapter 2," and after that, the simple words, "Be filled with the Holy Spirit."

"I have never heard anything like this before," George said to me as the room began to grow silent once more. I had to agree. All my life I had lived with a certain set of assumptions and, in a matter of weeks, they were all being swept away.

"They're so willing . . ." he continued, "so willing to do whatever it takes to find more of God!"

Father Dennis Bennett was the last speaker that night. This British-born Anglican minister had been the successful rector of a large Episcopal church in Southern California, until he received the Baptism in the Holy Spirit, in November 1959. For a while, he kept his own "personal Pentecost" to himself, but when he finally spoke about it to his congregation the following Easter, he launched a firestorm of controversy that put articles about "tongue-talking" on the pages of *Newsweek* and *Time*.

"There was nothing compulsive about tongues at all," Father Bennett continued. "It *was* a new language, not some kind of 'baby talk.' It had grammar and syntax, inflection and expression—and, if I may be so bold as to add," he said softly, "it was rather beautiful. My tongue tripped, just as it might when you are trying to recite a tongue twister," he said simply, "and I began to speak in a new language."

He made it sound so easy.

"Now, I know what some of you are thinking," he continued with a disarming smile, "because, *believe me*, I thought exactly the same thing: that this was some kind of psychological trick or form of compulsive behavior. After all, we have all been told, time and time again, by folk far more eloquent and educated than ourselves, that the power of the Holy Spirit—as it was poured out on the disciples in the book of Acts—is not available to us today. "But what about the power to witness to the lost?" His voice rose in a crescendo. "The power to stand up to temptation? The power to overcome? The power to change?" All around me, heads were nodding, some faces smiling, others frowning, deep in thought.

"Don't you think we need that power at work in our lives today?" he continued, forcefully driving home the point. "Or are we somehow better than the apostles?"

"What if he's telling the truth?" I kept thinking.

"Jesus describes the Holy Spirit, in John 16, with a Greek word—*paraklete*—a helper, a comforter, an advocate: someone called to come alongside the believer. He's the friend who will never leave you, the one who will convict you of sin, who'll teach you about righteousness and prepare you to stand on the Day of Judgment. He'll guide you into all truth, He'll prepare you for the days to come, and He'll reveal Jesus more fully to you."

"What would happen to the Church," he whispered dramatically into the microphone, "if we dared to believe these words of Jesus and walk in the power of the living God?"

There was a stunned silence.

"What would happen to you?" He held the entire auditorium in his steady, unflinching gaze.

"Jesus said, 'you will receive power when the Holy Spirit comes on you; and you will be my witnesses in Jerusalem, and in all Judea and Samaria, and to the ends of the earth.'"

"Yes," he said, passionately, "even *you!*"

My mind was spinning as I tried to process all that I had heard. What's more, Father Bennett had just invited anyone who wanted to receive the Baptism of the Holy Spirit to join him in the adjacent room.

I had a decision to make.

"What would happen to me if I said yes?" I kept thinking over and over again. "What would I be missing if I said no?"

Gradually, our group got up from the meeting and filtered out into the noise of the crowded lobby. I followed, just a few steps behind.

Suddenly, Velma spoke out, clearly, for all of us to hear: "I would like to go into that room!" she said, her uncharacteristic boldness catching me by surprise.

"So would I!" added George, just as loudly.

I turned to speak to him, shocked at what I heard. I knew deep in my heart that I needed to go, too, but we hadn't even had a chance to talk.

"George. Wait!"

But he was already gone, striding ahead through the crowd. One thing was certain: If George spoke in tongues, it was real—he was *never* given to emotional experiences. I rushed after him. By the time I got there, about thirty people were gathered in the prayer room, kneeling in a circle, as they had been directed. I quietly slipped in and stood behind George.

"There is nothing difficult about this," Father Bennett was already explaining. "I'm just going to come around and pray for you one by one. Be willing to receive, just as the Holy Spirit ministers to you."

George was certainly willing. His eyes were closed and he was lost in silent prayer when Father Bennett came up to him and placed his hands on his head.

"Receive the Holy Spirit," he prayed, very simply and gently, without a lot of show or ceremony. He then reached over to me and prayed the exact same thing. As I shut my eyes, the fear and anticipation churned together inside. I listened and waited.

Several minutes went by. A low murmur spread across the room. Some people were weeping quietly, others were beginning to pray softly.

Then I opened my eyes in astonishment. Something

was happening to George.

It looked like him and sounded like him, but it was unlike anything I had ever witnessed. He was praying in a language I had never heard before. Could it be real? I stole a quick glance at Velma. It looked like something similar was happening to her! She had her hands raised in the air and there was such joy on her face. Gradually, others started speaking around the room: different voices and different sounds, combining together in a chorus so foreign, yet so glorious, it seemed as though the angels in heaven were joining in.

It must be real! Yet nothing was happening to me. I looked at the floor, not wanting to make eye contact with anyone. Although I was standing in the same room and had been prayed for just like the others, I wasn't kneeling and I wasn't experiencing what they were. I was on the outside and had no idea how to enter in.

I remembered my parents. My father had a profound faith in God. As a young man, he had had a vision of hell, and it impacted his life from then on. Spiritual things were real to him; he saw them clearly. My mother, on the other hand, struggled with her faith.

And as I stood there that night, I wondered if perhaps I was more like my mother.

"Maybe it isn't for everyone," I thought.

By the time we rejoined our group, they were sitting in the hotel coffee shop eating dessert, curiously awaiting the news. They gathered around the three of us, paying particular attention to George.

"It was as though a ball of emotion was rising from deep inside me," he shared. "It moved up through my chest and then erupted into words that I couldn't understand."

As the conversation lulled, George glanced over, appearing to notice me for the first time. "What about *you*, Betty?"

"I . . . I guess . . . I didn't really feel anything." I stammered, lowering my eyes. "Nothing happened."

Those were the last words I spoke for quite some time.

But George could tell that *something* had happened as we drove away that night. The stony look on my face, however, kept him from asking any questions. As we got ready for bed, the silence got worse. I wasn't interested in following our normal pattern of praying together before sleep. I just lay there, quiet and unresponsive, my thoughts getting more and more out of control. Was George going on ahead? Was I being left behind spiritually—far behind?!

I turned on my side and pulled the covers with me. How would the Baptism of the Holy Spirit *change* my husband? Why would God give something to him, only to withhold it from me?

As the hours slowly ticked by, my imagination ran wild. I could tell I was keeping George awake, but I didn't care. Something dark and uncontrollable was rising up inside me and I didn't even have the desire to resist it.

Then a thought came to my mind. "You're threatened by him yielding to Me, because you're not fully yielded yourself."

I would like to think that I listened to those words, but I was too upset to recognize that they came from the Lord. So neither George, nor I, slept much that night. I tossed and turned, depressed and resentful and, as the night wore on, became more upset.

• • •

"I'M NOT GOING to church today," I announced the next morning, as George stood in the bathroom, straightening his tie in the mirror. "The boys can stay home with me." He looked at me, astonished, and opened his mouth. I braced myself for a fight. But then, surprisingly, his response never came. He just turned his back.

"All right, Betty" he said with a sigh, and walked away down the hallway.

The day passed even more slowly, and staying home from church didn't help. I was tired and irritable around the children. For his part, George was clearly distressed by the tension.

It was late afternoon when the phone rang.

"Hi Betty, it's Dot. George said you were having a hard time. Just wanted you to know that we're all praying for you!"

I put the phone down.

"George! Did you talk about me at Sunday school?"

"I just told Bud and Dot that we both needed some prayer," he said, a guilty look spreading across his face.

"And why is that exactly?" I shot back.

"Betty. You're all worked up about the Holy Spirit, and I just don't know what to do."

"Oh, am I?" I yelled, storming off into the bedroom and slamming the door.

Evening fell before George suggested we go for a visit to Bud and Dot's house. Within an hour, we both found ourselves sitting on the couch in their living room.

"Betty, my dear, what's wrong?" Dot asked kindly, as she brought in some refreshments on a tray.

"Can I be perfectly honest with you?" I asked hesitantly. They nodded.

"I feel that God has rejected me!"

Bud smiled, reassuringly, and didn't say a word. I watched him walk over to the stereo, open the lid, and flip on the power.

What was he doing? I wondered, as he carefully dropped a crackling needle onto the record spinning below. The simple organ melody gave way to a man's voice, strong, deep, and resonant. It was George Beverly Shea, the well-known soloist who traveled the nation singing at Billy Graham's gospel crusades. It was his song, "The Love of God" that broke through my depression that day.

The love of God is greater far
Than tongue or pen can ever tell;
It goes beyond the highest star,
And reaches to the lowest hell;
O love of God, how rich and pure!
How measureless and strong!
It shall for evermore endure
The saints' and angels' song.

"You know," Bud said, lifting the needle as the music ended, "God's love will reach you even in your place of despair. He hasn't left you or forgotten you. He is a loving Father and He seeks good gifts for you. You just need to go back to His Word. Get out your Bible and seek Him for yourself. If you seek Him, you will find Him."

• • •

AS THE WEEK WENT BY, Bud's words stayed with me. Whenever I had a spare moment, I would get out the Bible and search through the scriptures to learn more about the Holy Spirit. And the more I did, the more I began to embrace the infectious excitement that seemed to grip George.

"Hey, Betty," he said later that week, bursting excitedly into the room, "I was just driving down the street thanking God, and I started speaking in another language!"

About an hour or so later, he was back.

"Betty Joyce!" he called, running through the house, looking for me. "Betty Joyce!!

"I just finished at the McAlister Stables, and it happened again. It sounded like Chinese! And I spoke it all the way to my next appointment! I feel so close to God." It didn't stop. All afternoon, as he came back between his country calls, the same thing would happen again and again: seven times in one day, same story, different languages—languages George had never studied or spoken before.

He lay there, stretched out on the bed that night, hands tucked behind his head, thinking out loud. "Betty, what do you think it means?"

I stopped brushing my teeth and shrugged my shoulders. I was just as interested to know as he was.

"Do you think, perhaps, we are going to go to all those nations someday?"

"Us?" I smiled. "George, we have never even been out of the States."

• • •

SIX WEEKS PASSED, and I was determined to keep seeking the Lord. I read through the book of Acts and the book of Romans and had nearly finished the Gospels when, one morning, I came upon a verse that set me free.

Then John gave this testimony: "I saw the Spirit come down from heaven as a dove and remain on him [Jesus]. I would not have known him, except that the one who sent me to baptize with water told me, 'The man on whom you see the Spirit come down and remain is he who will baptize with the Holy Spirit.' I have seen and I testify that this is the Son of God."
(John 1:32–34 NIV1984)

Once I saw that Jesus Himself would be the one to baptize me, the fear that had so gripped me left and I began to love Him all the more. It had nothing to do with anyone else: Jesus was the Baptizer, not me, not George, not even Dennis Bennett! I could expect the experience to come straight from Him.

One night, I was home by myself; George was making some evening calls at the stables out along the canal. The boys were asleep, and I had just finished cleaning up the kitchen.

"One more load in the washing machine," I thought to myself, "and then I'll be able to sit down and read." The more I read, the more I yearned to spend time in my Bible each day.

So I quickly gathered up the laundry and practically ran down the basement stairs, dropping a trail of socks and washcloths behind me. There, in the quietness of the evening, as I bent forward to turn the dial and listen to the cold water rush in, I heard myself speaking in tongues.

"George, George!" I called out, flinging open the front door as soon as I heard his footsteps on the porch, "Jesus filled me with the Holy Spirit! I was speaking in tongues and I didn't even know it!"

• • •

IN A FEW SHORT WEEKS, during the spring of 1966, the Baptism of the Holy Spirit swept through our Bible study like wildfire. One night, we met at Bob and Sherry's house and so many came forward wanting individual prayer that we quickly ran out of room. In the end, George and I found ourselves taking some people into the bathroom, the only remaining space available. What a sight to remember as they knelt there before God, weeping by the commode. Thirteen people received the Baptism that night. It was one-thirty in the morning by the time we got home. George was beside himself with excitement.

"We have to tell someone!" he said, picking up the telephone to call Neil and Velma, who had missed the meeting because of work. "I'm not going to wait till tomorrow."

A few days later, *my* opportunity to tell someone came. George had already left for the racetracks, and I was in the kitchen making breakfast for the children, humming softly in my newfound prayer language.

"Mother?"

I glanced up, startled. I hadn't realized that Allen had been watching me.

"I'm sorry, Allen. What is it?"

"Mother, *what* has happened to you and Daddy?" he asked. "You're so different."

I took the eggs off the burner and turned off the stove. "Allen, come here." I looked into his eyes. "We have invited Jesus to come into our lives. He's forgiven us and made us new—in here!" I pointed to my heart.

"Allen," I told him very simply, "Jesus changes everything!"

"Could He change me too?" he asked.

"Of course He can!" I replied. "Would you like to invite Him into your heart?"

"Yes."

"Right now?"

He nodded.

So as we knelt together on the kitchen floor, I led Allen in a salvation prayer.

"I'm a sinner, I need a Savior," he said, repeating the phrases after me, his eyes shut tight with all the seriousness he could muster. "Come into my life, Lord Jesus."

My eyes filled with tears and I marveled at God. Less than a year ago, I had whispered a cry to the heavens. And here I was, teaching Allen, the first of my children, to know Jesus. God had been Faithful!

A few days later, Father Dennis Bennett returned. Bud and Dot had invited him to stay for the weekend and speak to our home-group. By Sunday evening, Allen wanted to know more. George and I were sitting at the dinner table, fervently discussing all we had heard, when he interrupted us both in mid-sentence.

"Can He fill me too?" he spoke up, as if he were asking the question to himself.

"What do you mean?" I asked, looking across the table in surprise.

"With the Holy Spirit," said Allen. "Is this just for adults?"

"Of course it's for everyone," I replied without thinking, before realizing, as I did, that I wasn't really sure. "George?" I looked at him over Allen's head.

"What about Dennis Bennett?" George asked. "He would know. And he might still be with the Cobbs."

Early the next morning, we called Bud's house to see if Father Bennett was still there. "If so", George asked, "would he be willing to pray for Allen to receive the Baptism of the Holy Spirit?"

"Yes—by all means," came the response.

So George and Allen left the house, earlier than usual, stopping in on Bud and Dot on the way to school.

The day passed slowly.

"Mother, *Mother!*" My heart leapt at the sound of

Allen's voice as he rushed through the back door later that afternoon. "Mother, you were right," he said breathlessly, his words tumbling out in a torrent. "Father Bennett was at home. We saw him. I knelt down in the den and he prayed for me just like you and Daddy said he would."

"And what happened after that?" I asked, feeling the thrill of his excitement.

"I don't really know," he said, after a moment's thought. "But the sky is bluer, the grass is greener, and I have been speaking in Spanish all day!"

Scan this code with your camera-equipped smartphone to view the companion video for Chapter Five. If you do not have the QR app on your phone, visit your app store and search for *QR code reader.*

SIX

Do You Appreciate What George Does for You?

The wise woman builds her house, but with her own hands the foolish one tears hers down.
Proverbs 14:1 (NIV)

All around me, the house was unusually quiet. It was almost eight o'clock in the morning; George had left for the racetracks not long after dawn and Allen was already on his way to school. For once, the younger boys were sleeping in.

I picked up my coffee and walked slowly through our new home, humming quietly to myself, determined to savor the moment before the silence was broken. Out of the living room window, I could see the strengthening rays of the late summer sun lighting up the tropical plants and young palms that were dotted across the neatly trimmed front lawn. It was truly beautiful.

We had moved out of Ives Dairy in June of that year and bought the builder's model home on Jackson Street, just a few minutes' walk from Bud and Dot Cobb's house.

In many ways, it was the consummation of my Florida dream: living in the heart of Hollywood Hills, in a brand new subdivision, with a year-round lawn service and a sprinkler system so advanced that it could be turned on, day or night, with the simple flick of a switch.

I stepped into the den and sank gratefully into one of the overstuffed armchairs that we had just bought from the Ethan Allen showroom in Fort Lauderdale. The whole family had gone there a week earlier and George and I had picked out a roomful of furniture.

And I loved it.

I leaned back and sipped my coffee, thinking back to the scene in this room the previous night. It was Sunday evening, and the family had stayed up late, watching one of the many biblical epics that became so popular in the 1950s and '60s. Phillip and Allen were each curled up in the chairs, fighting to stay awake for fear of being carried off to bed, like Doyle; hoping that George and I wouldn't notice as we sat on the couch.

It was the climax of the movie, and I was transfixed. Jesus was hanging on the cross surrounded by chisel-faced Roman soldiers and sobbing women. He was dead, and his battered, lifeless body was lowered in a sheet and carried to a nearby tomb. The dramatic strains of the orchestral score rose again to one final crescendo as the blackened screen lit up to reveal the lone, sobbing figure of Mary Magdalene, staring in disbelief as she emerged from the empty tomb into the bright sunlight of the rocky hillside. Her eyes caught sight of a man—the gardener—walking up the hill, a short distance away. She ran after him, tears still flowing down her face.

"Sir, Sir!" Mary called out, but the man continued walking. "Sir! Have you hidden him?! Tell me where and I will take him away."

"Woman, why do you weep?" came the gentle reply as the gardener stopped, his back turned from her.

"Because you have taken away my Lord. I know not where."

The man turned to face her.

"Magdalena," came his reply.

I gasped as the music swelled.

"It's Jesus!" I screamed as I leapt off the couch onto my feet, even before the on-screen Mary had a chance to respond. The boys jerked awake, startled by my outburst.

"You look more surprised than Mary," laughed George.

"He's so real!" I exclaimed.

When He turned, I had recognized that it was Jesus, just like Mary, and the powerful reality of His resurrection remained with me even now as I sat with my coffee in the den.

Suddenly, my dream came back to me in a rush. I had been so preoccupied remembering the movie that the dream, which had awakened me early that morning, had all but faded from my mind. But now it came back, flooding in with no warning, just as vividly as the night before. Then I remembered the words: "Be clean." They were similar to those I heard that November day while washing dishes in the kitchen sink: "I am the Truth," and they reminded me of the voice of the gardener in the film the night before.

I had no idea what *Be clean* meant.

Who could I ask? George, like me, was a beginner on this journey, and so were all our other friends in the Bible study group. Bud might know, I supposed, but he would always tell us, "I'm teaching you this week what I learned last week," as we gathered in his house each Monday night. I respected Bud, but I knew I needed someone more mature this time, someone who had walked with God much longer.

"Who, Lord? Who can help me be clean?" I whispered aloud, the urgency of my spoken prayer breaking the silence in the room. In that instant, I remembered the distinctive face of a woman clearly in my mind: Ruth Coffey.

Ruth and her husband were former missionaries to Cuba who now lived in Coral Gables, half an hour down the freeway in the southern part of Miami. She was in her late forties, with fine features and striking red hair, a remarkable Christian woman with six children and little money who, nevertheless, always looked as though she had just stepped out of a beauty parlor. Ruth was not a person you could easily forget.

Nor was her story.

Forced to flee after the Communist revolution, the Coffeys had spent the past five or six years speaking in home groups and church meetings up and down the Florida coast. Wherever they went, Ruth raised awareness of the plight of the Cuban church that had been driven deep underground following Fidel Castro's vow to rid the island of religion.

The first time we met, I went straight up to her. She had just finished sharing her story at a meeting we attended, and it had left a powerful impression on me. I had never before heard of persecuted Christians laying down their lives in a simple effort to live out their faith, and I sensed that Ruth Coffey was a woman with much more to teach. So I had gathered up my courage and asked for her number; it had sat by the telephone ever since.

My excitement growing, I saw the slip of paper just waiting to be found. I was amazed at God, that He was willing to speak in so many different ways.

Picking up the receiver, I started to dial the number: my fingers catching each new digit and dragging it around the face of the phone before the mechanism even had a chance to spring back into place. I heard a loud click as the line connected, and then a distant ring.

"Good morning, Ruth Coffey speaking," the voice at the other end said brightly.

"Mrs. Coffey," I began, "this is Betty Jackson. I met you at the conference a few weeks back."

Her response was friendly. "Of course, I remember you, Betty," she laughed. "You were the new believer sitting up at the front. How are you?"

"I had this dream last night," I said, sensing the invitation to jump straight in. "God spoke to me and told me to be clean. The thing is, Mrs. Coffey . . ."

"Betty, dear," she replied kindly, "please call me Ruth."

"Thank you," I said. "The thing is, Ruth, I just don't know what that means. And since you were the first one who came to mind when I was praying this morning, I thought perhaps you might be someone who could help?"

"This *has* to be the Lord!" she exclaimed. "I think you need to meet Aunt Mary."

"Who is Aunt Mary?" I asked, intrigued.

"Mary Booth," she continued, "is one of a kind. She was a missionary we got to know during our time in Cuba. And she just happens to be arriving from Oregon today. She'll know exactly how to help you. In fact, I'm picking her up from the bus station in a few minutes. Isn't the Lord good?"

"Well, in that case—" I said, quickly mapping out the week ahead. It was Monday today; I could easily organize a lunch meeting for Friday . . . Sherry, Marie, Velma, and the rest of the "girls" would probably like to hear her as well. "—would she be able to come to my house for lunch and speak to a few women in our Bible Study?" I was eager not to waste another minute.

• • •

BY FRIDAY NOON, almost fifty women were gathered in our living room, each carrying a covered dish. News that Ruth Coffey was bringing a missionary from Cuba to Betty's new home on Jackson Street spread like wildfire, far beyond the immediate circle of Bud's Bible study. As the week went on, the guest list grew steadily.

"You know Betty," Sherry joked as we tried to squeeze another chair in the hallway, "you would have been in big trouble if you had tried to keep all this excitement to yourself!"

Phillip stood in the middle of the room, looking quite adorable with his closely cropped blonde hair and shining blue eyes, captivating the assembled company with his repertoire of Sunday school songs and clearly gaining momentum from the crowd as he did. Over in the far corner, Doyle was happily playing on the floor with Karen Feller, Nadine's baby girl, some nine months younger, pulling a blanket on and off her head repeatedly for comic effect. There was an unusual amount of chatter and expectation, even though there was still no sign of Ruth or her mysterious guest.

That's when Nadine came up to me, quietly standing

by the doorway.

"The pastor wrote a letter to Bob," she said softly, bringing my thoughts back to Earth. "It just came in the mail yesterday."

"What did it say?" I asked, sensing her distress.

"They don't want him reading the Scripture portion anymore."

"What do you mean?" I asked, puzzled. Bob was a radio announcer by profession and read the Bible beautifully. He was considered one of the pillars of Hollywood Hills Methodist Church.

"He has a choice," Nadine continued. "Give up the Monday night study or lose his position in the church. They said they don't want this Holy Spirit craze spreading any further."

I wondered what Bob had done wrong. George and I didn't have any formal role at church with all the busyness of work and the boys, but most of our friends in the Bible study did. What about them? Were they in trouble too?

I had no time to respond to Nadine. Doyle started getting restless across the room, and as I picked him up into my arms, I heard a knock on the door.

"Sorry we're a little late," said Ruth Coffey as I ushered her into the crowded hallway. "Betty, let me introduce you to Mary Booth."

I don't know why, but I had imagined that a frontline missionary who had stood up for the Cuban Christians against the persecution of the Communist authorities would be a large, intimidating woman with an unshakeable air of authority. Mary Booth, however, was nothing like that. She was petite and fragile, with large oversized glasses, platform shoes, and a brown wig; she seemed quirky, perhaps even a little eccentric, but she was an obvious magnet to the younger women, who now gathered around her, pressed together on every available inch of carpet that was not already occupied by a chair.

She took a seat at the far end of the living room and, after a short time, began to speak, even though the chatter of the women continued for a moment or two. I stood in the doorway, holding Doyle and looking on.

"I want to share with you a lesson I have learned," she began gently, forcing me to strain forward to catch her softly spoken words. "The Bible calls it 'overcoming,' and we are *all* told to overcome: whether it is the sin in our lives or our difficult circumstances, Jesus is bigger than both." She paused and looked around. "Isn't Jesus wonderful?"

We all nodded, a little taken aback by the simple intimacy of those words. It was obvious that she was no ordinary Sunday school teacher. "And when Jesus speaks to the seven churches in the book of Revelation," she continued, "He promises a blessing to *everyone* who overcomes."

There was a moment's silence as she started turning through the pages of her Bible, repeatedly pushing her glasses back into place. "Oh, my!" she exclaimed, as her eyes scanned the verses. "All of these Christians are in a pretty bad way, don't you think? Some have lost their first love. Some have fallen into sin. Some are suffering persecution. Yet Jesus makes a promise to them all. He will bless them if they overcome.

> *To him that overcometh will I grant to sit with me in my throne, even as I also overcame, and am set down with my Father in his throne. He that hath an ear, let him hear what the Spirit saith unto the churches. "* (Revelation 3:21–22)

Mary's eyes shone brightly. "What do you suppose we have to overcome today? Why don't we listen to what the Spirit is saying to us?"

She began to recite by heart.

> *Now the works of the flesh are manifest, which are these; Adultery, fornication, uncleanness, lasciviousness, Idolatry, witchcraft, hatred, variance, emulations, wrath, strife, seditions, heresies, Envyings, murders, drunkenness, revellings, and such like: of the which I tell you before, as I have also told you in time past, that they which do such things shall not inherit the kingdom of God.* (Galatians 5:19–21)

By now she had everyone's attention and she began to read again, this time from Romans, chapter 6.

> *Knowing this, that our old man is crucified with him, that the body of sin might be destroyed, that henceforth we should not serve sin.*

"The key to our overcoming is found in this verse. Now, who do you suppose is your old man?"

There was a long, awkward silence.

"Isn't it the person I was before I met Jesus?" I suggested eagerly, standing on my tiptoes to see over the heads of the women gathered in the back of the room.

"That's right, Betty," Mary said, looking straight at me. "Before we met Jesus, we were slaves to sin. We had no ability to change. But meeting Jesus isn't the end of our struggle; in fact, it's quite the opposite. Paul himself tells us right here in the next chapter:

> *For I know that in me (that is, in my flesh,) dwelleth no good thing: for to will is present with me; but how to perform that which is good I find not. For the good that I would I do not: but the evil which I would not, that I do. Now if I do that I would not, it is no more I that do it, but sin that dwelleth in me.* (Romans 7:18–20)

"Paul still had to deal with *his* old man, just like the rest of us. He planted churches and preached the gospel, but he had to overcome the sinful nature that lived inside of him."

There was complete silence in the room, except for the rustling of pages and the cooing of baby Karen, in the corner on the floor. Mary's thin voice continued, "Isn't it encouraging to know that Paul struggled with sin, too? There was a part of him that got angry and wanted to fight back; that got anxious and wanted to fall into fear. I think there was also a part of him that got lonely and wanted to give in to temptation.

"He understood something that is very important," she continued, pausing a moment as if to gather her thoughts. "When we give in to our selfish desires—even though we are Christians—we once again become slaves, slaves to our problems and to our sins. And the only way out of slavery is to die! Our sinful, selfish nature must be put to death."

"Put to death?" I thought to myself, puzzled as to why a God who just earlier that week had told me to be clean would first want me to die. All around me the other women looked up, their surprise, like mine, mixed with a measure of confusion. None of us had ever heard these passages taught quite like *this* before.

"Paul says in Romans 6 that *'he who has died has been freed from sin.'*" She looked down at her Bible again. "And he carries on a few verses later with this:

*Likewise reckon ye also yourselves to be dead
indeed unto sin, but alive unto God through
Jesus Christ our Lord.* (Romans 6:11)

"I have a question for you," Mary said, looking around
at us with a disarming smile. "How can we live a life that
pleases God? How did Paul live to please Him?"

All around me were blank faces.

"Well, my Bible tells me that he counted himself dead
to sin. He realized that if he wanted to grow up in God,
he would first have to die. And if *Paul* had to die, then I
think you and I do too.

"If we don't put to death our hatred, our rage, our self-
ishness, and our envy, we won't 'inherit the kingdom of
God'! But if we die to ourselves, we receive the power of
Christ to live in step with the Spirit of God. Listen to this:

*But the fruit of the Spirit is love, joy, peace,
longsuffering, gentleness, goodness, faith,
meekness, temperance: against such there is no
law. And they that are Christ's have crucified the
flesh with the affections and lusts. If we live in
the Spirit, let us also walk in the Spirit.*
(Galatians 5:22–25)

"Isn't that good news?" she said, smiling. All around

her, fifty women sat bewildered, not so sure.

In all my years, I had never heard anyone speak of the apostle Paul as though they *knew* him; as though he were an everyday Christian who lived a life we could relate to. Aunt Mary was the first—probably because she had to learn these same lessons the hard way for herself. Widowed with a young daughter at only thirty years old, she assumed sole responsibility for her husband's filling station, in far tougher economic times than these. As I strained to hear her quiet voice, it became clear that the authority in her words did not come from any personal charisma; it was from the power of having lived out what she taught.

"So, how do *you* overcome?" she said, as she concluded. "It's simple. Lay down your sinful reactions: your rights, your desires, even your passions! Jesus plainly told his disciples:

> *Then said Jesus unto his disciples, if any man*
> *will come after me, let him deny himself, and*
> *take up his cross, and follow me.*
> (Matthew 16:24)

"Repent and confess your sin. When we take our old man to the Cross and repent, we receive the power to live in step with the Spirit of God, to be truly free to follow where Christ leads. Following Jesus requires me to encounter the cross again and again."

And as quickly and unexpectedly as she had begun, Aunt Mary was finished. Two or three of the young women sitting nearby began to ask her questions, while most of the others apologetically grabbed their purses and left.

"What if I don't want to die?" Sherry said with a smile as she got ready to leave. "Crucifixion sounds a little drastic, don't you think?"

"It does. But I'm not sure we have a choice," I replied earnestly.

And I honestly wasn't sure I did. Verses that had always just been words suddenly began to take on new meaning. If I wanted to live for Christ, I had to be willing to die to myself. I just didn't know what that looked like.

About thirty minutes later, the crowd had thinned down to only a few ladies. Phillip was playing happily in his room and Doyle, exhausted by all the attention and excitement, had gone down for an early afternoon nap.

Aunt Mary and Ruth were standing in the kitchen, alone. I realized that this was my opportunity and I didn't know if I would get another.

"Thank you so much for coming," I said gratefully. "I was wondering, do you have to leave yet, Aunt Mary?"

She looked at Ruth, then back at me.

"What's on your mind, Betty?"

"Well, I was wondering if you would spend the night here with us," I said. "I would like to learn more, and

I would really like my husband to meet you. I think he would value the opportunity to get to know you."

"Let me think about it," she responded, before closing her eyes momentarily. I watched, curiously.

"I would be happy to do that," she said after a while, "but you're not going to learn much in just one night. Perhaps I could stay a few more days?"

• • •

"THE BOYS ARE FINALLY ASLEEP," I said with a sigh, as I walked down the hallway into the kitchen at the end of the day. Aunt Mary had returned earlier in the evening, suitcase in hand, and was now walking through the house with a thoughtful look on her face, looking at the pictures and running her fingers admiringly along various pieces of furniture scattered from room to room.

"May I get you something to drink?" I asked, inviting her to take a seat at the kitchen table.

"Yes, dear," she replied kindly, "just hot water with a dash of cider vinegar. Keeps me healthy," she explained.

I poured the strong-smelling vinegar-water into one of my best china tea cups and sat down across from her. I knew her message of overcoming was the answer to my dream, but I had no idea how to apply it. In fact, I had no idea where to begin.

Mary just sat there in silence, running her fingers over

the wrought iron leaves that supported the smooth glass table top, clearly appreciating the quality of the finish and design.

"This is a nice table," she smiled warmly.

"Thank you, we just bought it."

"Hmmm."

The shrill ring of the telephone broke the silence.

"Excuse me, Mary," I said as I got up to answer it.

"Hello, this is Betty . . . When?! Oh." I glanced at the clock. "Okay, George," I sighed.

I sat back down and forced a smile, trying to cover my disappointment.

"Betty, does your husband normally get home at this time?" Aunt Mary asked.

"Yes. George has a very demanding job as a veterinarian," I explained.

"Oh. He works very hard!" She quietly observed. On that point, there was no question. His salary proved it, tripling in less than two years.

"Yes. I suppose so. A bit *too hard* perhaps. He's a good father, a wonderful husband, and a great provider for the family, but sometimes I think he's obsessed with his horses," I said. "That's the truth! It would be good if he could hear the message you gave this afternoon."

"Really?" Mary just sat there, listening.

"I can remember coming home from the hospital with Phillip," I continued, plunging ahead. "I had just given birth in Kansas City, and we were driving back to our house in Columbia, three hours away. About halfway home, George drove off a side road into the country. There was a mare for sale, which he examined and bought, right there and then. A horse?! Phillip was just ten days old, and all he could think of was buying a horse!" My tone was rising, and the frustration was beginning to show.

"A few weeks later, we loaded up the station wagon and drove more than eight hours to Middle Tennessee *just* so he could attend the Walking Horse Celebration. It was August, the height of summer. Phillip was six weeks old and had an elevated temperature with a bad case of diarrhea. I was awake all through the night giving him water from a dropper! And now . . ."

"Betty," Aunt Mary said softly, "do you appreciate what George does for you?"

I stopped cold. Appreciate what?

"Do you ever rub his feet at night when he gets home and is tired?"

"Rub his feet?!" I felt my face flush red. After taking care of three boys all day?! Cleaning the house? Making his dinner?! Now I was angry.

Gently, she put her hand on mine. "Betty, why don't we talk to the Lord about this?"

She prayed about everything! I was mad but strangely impressed at the same time. Without waiting for another word from me, she bowed her head and prayed quietly to herself, her lips barely moving. This continued for several minutes before she lifted her head. "Is it possible you have some resentment toward George? Betty, are you aware of the passage of Scripture in Proverbs 14:1? *'The wise woman builds her house, but with her own hands the foolish one tears hers down.'*"

I was unprepared for her truthfulness. My heart began to beat faster; my raw emotions were suddenly exposed. It was true. I was angry and bitter that he seemed to be more interested in his horses than in me. And I resented feeling like I was taking a back seat in his life. I could see it all now seething inside: the anger and criticism, the stubbornness and control. I had it all, and I recoiled at the thought.

"Do you know what the book of Hebrews says about bitterness?" she asked softly.

I shook my head. "I don't really care!"

Aunt Mary looked away, then she continued as if she hadn't heard me. "See to it that no one falls short of the grace of God and that no bitter root grows up to cause trouble and defile many," she recited. "A bitter root produces pride, animosity, rivalry—and many other things that can harm the people around you. We need to dig it out!" She bowed her head for several minutes.

My words still echoed in the air. Did I mean that? Could my attitude really affect my children?

A moment later, Aunt Mary looked up, smiling. "I just

saw a picture of George running after his horses. You're running too; George is far ahead of you."

I didn't quite understand what she meant by seeing a picture, but the image she described was so powerful that I could imagine it. It was quite a sight—me, five feet tall, running through a field after George who, in turn, was being outpaced by a couple of galloping horses.

Somehow, I knew Mary loved me and wanted me to understand what it meant to be clean. I also knew that what she was telling me was the absolute truth. I saw that I had a choice and there were two paths I could take. I could cause trouble and defile the whole family, or I could listen to what Mary was seeking to teach me.

"But how do I really change?" I swallowed quickly, my eyes welling up with tears of shame.

"Betty, you start by thanking God for George."

"For George?" I could feel it rising up again, that old carnal nature rearing its head.

"Of course. It is the cost of following Jesus. Thankfulness changes you. It's not going to change George, but it will change you. And Betty, listen to me: it will change your children too. If you resent your husband, you will cause your children to resent both you and your husband."

"But what about him?" I complained, wondering why this whole message of overcoming depended so much on me.

"You can't pick green fruit," Mary chuckled. "If you

pick fruit too early, it will just spoil. People have to be desperate before you can help them. Okay now, what about *you?* Are you desperate, or are we finished?"

I could feel the struggle intensifying inside as I weighed the choice. The old Betty wanted to chase George down and make him change. But there was something simple in Mary's invitation: an invitation to stop running and start *yielding,* trusting God to change *me,* to die to *myself* and live for Christ. What would a new Betty look like? I didn't know.

"Okay," I said finally. I knew it wasn't just Mary who was waiting, I could sense that God was waiting too. "I'm ready."

"Let's put this resentment on the cross," she said, "and repent of it! Why don't you repeat this prayer after me? Heavenly Father, I thank you for my husband."

"Heavenly Father, I thank you for my husband," I echoed.

"I take my anger and resentment to the cross and I repent of it. I thank you Father that through Jesus Christ, I can be changed. Please forgive me for my stubbornness, rebellion, and my unwillingness to change. I have been so wrong, but I want to be different. I thank you that when I come to you, in humility, Father, You do forgive me and You will change me. Help me to honor and respect my husband."

I repeated each phrase, word for word, then took a

deep breath and burst into tears.

"There we are, dear," she patted my hand. "There it goes!"

I couldn't see anything, but I could feel it leave. I felt relief and refreshingly new.

"Now, I want you to write these steps in your Bible. They will help you remember how to take it to the cross:

> One: Thank Him for your circumstances, He's using them to purify you.

> Two: Thank Him for the person God is using in your life to rid you of your own selfish self. For most of us, that's the person closest to us.

> Three: We need to name our sin. What is it? Anger? Pride? Unforgiveness? Name it out loud.

> Four: Repent. The Bible says, "If we confess our sins, He is faithful and just to forgive us our sins and to cleanse us from all unrighteousness." True beauty, Betty, is defined by what you learn at the foot of the Cross.

> Five: Ask God to fill the empty space with

His Spirit. Don't just put off the old man, put on the new. Invite Him in. Receive His forgiveness, peace, and joy. Trust in the power of Jesus' blood. Be clean!"

All my life, I had seen the cross from a distance; how Jesus hung on it and shed His blood for our sins. But I never fully grasped the power it held until that day; that I could die to my sin and walk away free, overcoming my selfish desires standing steady, unwavering.

I knew now He wanted me to be clean. If I was willing to be honest with God and repent, He would change me.

Scan this code with your camera-equipped smartphone to view the companion video for Chapter Six. If you do not have the QR app on your phone, visit your app store and search for **QR code reader.**

SEVEN

May I Join You, Daddy?

*We were therefore buried with him through
baptism into death in order that...
we too may live a new life.*
Romans 6:4 (NIV)

I would like to think that I changed instantly after that first conversation with Aunt Mary, but I didn't. I found myself starting over every day, more determined, yet still giving in to the anger and resentment inside. The process was similar for George. He was greatly impacted by the week Aunt Mary spent with us on Jackson Street, but in the end he was not so very different. Days would pass in peace, we would pray, seek God together, read our Bibles, go to meetings and then the smallest trigger would start the cycle again.

It seemed like I was never going to get it. Honoring my husband was turning out to be one of the hardest things I had ever had to do.

"Oh," Aunt Mary would always say when I would call her from time to time, "I believe we need to pray about that again."

And then she would hand out the homework: "Betty, remember that God promises an inheritance to those who overcome. So you only have two options: either overcome or be overcome. Read Revelation 21:1–7. It will help you!"

A week or two later, we would be having the same conversation again.

"Betty, dying to self requires suffering. Peter tells us that Jesus suffered for our sins in His own body, that we must 'arm ourselves with the same attitude' and get ready to suffer too! That's how we can be free from our selfishness and sin: we crucify the flesh! It has to become a way of life. And it hurts, dear, I know. Read 1 Peter 4. The message of the cross is simple, Betty—but it isn't easy!"

She was right. It wasn't easy at all.

It was early summer in 1967, a year since my encounter with the Holy Spirit in the laundry room and almost two years since Doyle's birth. More and more of us began arriving at the Sunday services, clutching our treasured New Testaments, talking in animated voices about the truths we had uncovered together, as we had searched the Scriptures the week before. But what had begun as a ripple of suspicion in our home church in Hollywood Hills had gradually turned into a wave of hostility against Bud's Bible study.

At first, we thought it was a generational divide. Our group had grown to include a large cross-section of the younger couples in the church. But our hunger for the Scriptures was met with a measure of disapproval by the older folk, who would sit impassively on the front two rows. It soon became clear that our pastor, himself, was becoming increasingly exasperated with the situation.

Dr. Amos Boren, our pastor, was without doubt a great orator and thinker; a theologian of impeccable credentials. He could deliver a sermon in the finest English, filled with complex thoughts and ideas. He would weave the words of great philosophers, authors, and Bible commentators together in an intricate defense of his chosen biblical text. He made us think, challenged our presuppositions, and questioned everything so rigorously that, sometimes, we were left without even a kernel of belief to hold onto.

Yet for all Dr. Boren's intellect, something about our Bible study group challenged him.

"What has Buddy got that I haven't?" he asked Bob and Nadine Feller one day, agitated by their refusal to follow his advice and give up the group. "He's only a year or two older than you, and he has no formal religious education."

"I know," Bob replied humbly.

"What theological qualifications does he have?" Dr. Boren persisted. "What seminary did he attend?"

Bob was silent.

"Exactly," Dr Boren continued. "Don't you realize, Bob, how much I would love for you to be able to return to reading the Scripture lesson each week? You have a wonderful voice and you read so beautifully, but it is simply impossible for you to hold a position in this church as long as you are participating in this nonsense!"

The Fellers just nodded and responded as graciously as they could, just as Aunt Mary had taught them.

"We understand," Bob said quietly. "Thank you."

Not long after Bob's dismissal, our friends in the choir started to receive letters in the mail. The wording was a little different, but the ultimatum was the same: give up the Monday night Bible study or leave the choir.

"Sally," Dr. Boren told her when the time came for her to discuss her position in the choir, "why don't you turn your Bible to Mark, chapter 16, verse 9, and read it for me?"

She dutifully read all the way to verse 17, "*And these signs will accompany those who believe: In my name they will drive out demons, they will speak in new tongues . . .*" (NIV1984)

"You can stop there," Dr Boren instructed gently, before placing his copy of the Bible on the desk in front of her. "Now read those same verses, but this time from mine."

There was silence.

"Go on," he urged, "start at verse 9."

"But, Dr. Boren," Sally ventured falteringly, "there's nothing there!"

"Precisely," he replied, a hint of triumph in his voice.

"Do you know why? Because this translation is the work of true scholars, great men from Harvard, Yale, Johns Hopkins, and Vanderbilt. Believe me, they have cross-checked the ancient texts with recently discovered manuscripts, word by word and line by line. And those verses you read about demons and tongues? They are simply not there!"

"Sir," Sally replied softly, "I understand your feelings, but I'm learning so much at the Bible study. I'm growing in my faith—"

"But, you *don't* understand," Dr Boren interjected, getting increasingly animated, "Bud's an airline pilot! And he is telling you that you can trust every word you read in your Bible? Come on, Sally, I wish it was that simple, but it isn't!"

We only found out a few days later about Sally's encounter with the pastor. She was shaken and distressed.

"But, Betty," she said on the telephone one night, "What if Dr. Boren is right? He's an intelligent man, far more educated than the rest of us. He even knows Greek!"

My mind flashed back to that first day in Sunday school and the jaded voice of Dr. Boren's own daughter from the back of the room, shattering my newfound hope.

I paused for a moment. "Sally, has doubt been sown in your heart? Could your feelings be revealing something that *you* need to overcome?"

"I think you might be right, Betty," she gratefully replied.

"This may be a perfect example of what Aunt Mary has been teaching us."

It wasn't long before Bud and Dot were finally summoned before the church board.

"Bud, I appreciate you stepping in and leading the Sunday school when you did," Dr. Boren began sternly, without a hint of gratitude showing through. "But I'm afraid you simply cannot carry on any longer. This fervor about "tongues" is sweeping through our church, and rather than stopping it, you have deliberately encouraged it!" He spoke of "tongues" as though it were a bad word.

There was silence for a moment before he carried on.

"I'm responsible for this congregation, Bud, and you have been allowing this subjective emotionalism to take root like a cancer. It must be removed before it spreads any further. You are relieved of your duties here. Please leave, for all our sakes."

So one by one, we all left the church quietly, without argument or complaint, just as Aunt Mary had taught us.

"Leave, if you must," she would say to us when the topic of Dr. Boren came up. "But don't talk bad and don't talk back. Never be responsible for causing division in a church."

Our Bible study carried on, gathering together each week at Bud and Dot's home. We also attended the Full Gospel Businessmen's Fellowship and other teaching meetings that passed through the area from time to time, and life, in many ways, returned to normal. All of us battled through the rejection of the church in our own different ways: at least we had each other and we did our best to work through it.

For George and me, that meant moving on.

It was the busiest period of the Florida racetrack season, just a week or two before the thoroughbreds would head up north to their summer stables for the great New York races at Belmont, Long Island, and farther upstate in Saratoga Springs. One night, the food was already on the table and I didn't expect George to be home early. He had been home late from work every night that week and would probably be so until the annual stable migration was complete. I was even debating whether to set him a place at all as I brought the dishes from the kitchen to the dining room.

But Phillip, who was helping to arrange the silverware, was confident.

"Daddy will be home soon," he said. "He needs a place at the table, too."

Sure enough, just a few moments later, George burst in through the side door, unusually cheerful for that time of day.

"I have some good news," he announced. "Sit down. Sit down." He pulled out a chair for me, and the older boys crowded around while Doyle toddled forward, jostling past his brothers to find his way to the front.

"How would you like to live on a farm?" George asked enthusiastically, looking at the boys and then stooping down to pick up Doyle and place him on his knee. "With horses!"

"Real horses?" exclaimed Phillip, "Like Comanche Sue?"

"Yes. Real horses, just like Sue," George replied with a grin.

I looked up at his face nervously. Behind his black-rimmed glasses, his blue eyes danced with vision and belief. "I'm going to start my own practice—"

"Yeah!" Phillip interrupted merrily, young enough to be on board with anything his daddy suggested.

Allen looked surprised, grasping the significance of the statement a little more than his brother. "Are we moving, Mommy?" he asked.

"Do you remember New Year's Day?" continued George.

I couldn't forget it. George had found himself starting out the year on the side of the road, changing a flat tire. It was unseasonably warm, his family was at home, and there he was, trying to finish his rounds, sweat pouring down his face, struggling with a set of stubborn wheel nuts on the Palmetto Expressway. He came home that afternoon and didn't say a word. In fact, it took several days for him even to begin to share what was on his mind.

Would there ever be room for advancement with Dr.

Teigland? George loved the work and liked the people, but there was no guarantee that he would be invited to become a partner, at least not anytime soon. Sure, he had gained invaluable experience in his time at the racetracks, but for what? He was working almost eighty hours a week for someone else.

"My father used to tell me owning your own business is the most rewarding: to work for yourself and to set your own goals," George told me. "Maybe it's time for me to do the same."

So ever since the New Year, he had talked more seriously about starting his own practice, and his plan was beginning to take shape. George would be responsible for treating the animals, and I would be his office manager. After all, I had graduated as a medical secretary from business college and had worked some of the better jobs at the University of Missouri. He knew I was capable, and we could save a lot of money by working together. Yet I had always thought of this idea as more of a distant dream—somewhere down the road in five or ten years' time.

"I've done the research, Betty," he continued, jolting me back to the present. "And I have the experience. So I have filed for my license in Tennessee—"

"Tennessee?" I said, overwhelmed. He wanted to leave Florida?! Florida was my life! There were so many opportunities here!

"There's only one equine practice covering all of Middle

Tennessee," George continued. "We can move south of Nashville to Murfreesboro on Highway 41, close to the largest stables."

"We're moving to *Murfeesboo,*" Phillip shouted excitedly and danced around the table. "We're moving to *Murfeesboo!*"

Murfreesboro was a college town, surrounded by cotton fields and farms. It was small and rural. We had been there several times while living in Missouri in order to attend the local horse shows with my brother and his wife. Yet, as I had told Aunt Mary, I didn't have the best memories of the place: weekends in a cramped, hot hotel room with two young boys while George, already obsessed with horses, went out and looked at more.

"Oh, George!" I said, my eyes widening.

"Betty," George tried again, a little more gently this time, "I can work with American Saddlebreds, Hackneys, and Tennessee Walking Horses. It's going to be all right. Trust me. We'll go up there in a few weeks and buy a house, and then we'll start the clinic out of our home. Nearly all my work is out in the field; even here, in Florida, I use my station wagon as my office 95 percent of the time. No one will know, and if their horses are treated right, they won't care! The great thing is," he continued, his excitement building again, "we can take our time, find the perfect piece of land, and build a clinic on it and a home next door. The boys will get to grow up on a farm—it'll be great for them!"

"What about our house?" I asked. We had been in it less than a year!

"This is a great neighborhood," he said, undaunted. "It'll sell quick!"

"But what about our friends?" I continued, trying desperately to hold onto the people we had grown so close to.

"Betty, you make friends wherever you go," he replied. I thought of Sherry and Sally; Velma and Neil; Bud and Dot. "How do you know we'll find another Bible study in Murfreesboro?"

"Betty . . . God's also in Murfreesboro!" he said.

I gulped, recognizing the look in his eye. Ten years of marriage had taught me that when George set his mind on something, nothing would dissuade him from seeing it through.

And that was it. We were moving to Tennessee; the conversation was over. We ate the rest of our dinner in silence. Allen didn't say much, but Phillip chatted away happily about horses and sheep and cows, seemingly oblivious to the deepening tension that filled the room. I felt sick inside but left the table to get the boys ready for bed, masking my emotions. George went straight to the bedroom to get some peace and allow me time to process his plan.

Sometime later, I found myself back in the kitchen, distressed and confused, not knowing how to express all

that I felt. It was getting close to the time we would normally lie in bed and pray together, but I couldn't think of
anything that I felt less like doing.

"It's easy for George," I complained to God. "He can
just walk away from the Bible study, from Dr. Teigland,
from Hollywood Hills and leave them behind in a moment and not think twice."

I grabbed the last of the dinner dishes off the table and
put them in the dishwasher, hoping to buy myself a few
more minutes to think. The picturesque sight through the
kitchen window was not lost upon me: orange trees alight
with the last rays of the setting sun. I knew what lay behind George's decision. He didn't think that Miami, with
its sandy beaches and concrete sidewalks, was the best en-
vironment in which to rear the boys. He wanted them to
experience a small town upbringing, as he had during the
summers he had spent with his grandparents as a child.

But Florida was the epitome of the good life for me—
perfect for a young mother with three little boys. I had
tasted freedom here: freedom to stay home with the children without having to go to work; freedom from sickness
and the fear of impending death; and above all, freedom
in Christ—to learn and grow and find true meaning in my
life.

I wasn't so sure about Tennessee.

Suddenly, Aunt Mary's inquisitive face popped into
my mind. I slowly turned the faucet off and dropped my

dish cloth into the sink. If she were here, I thought, she would be looking at me right now saying, "Oh, my! Betty, shouldn't you talk to Jesus about what you're feeling right now?" My face flushed. I thought of all of our conversations about learning to take our sins to the cross. I remembered my own words just that past week to Sally. How quickly I had forgotten them!

I set the plates down and my eyes started to fill with tears. I sank to my knees and lay prostrate, hands stretched out in front of me, on the hard, yellow terrazzo floor. I pressed my forehead against its coldness—humbling myself as best I could.

I desperately wanted to be open to God's will, yet how could I change *mine*? "My will is so strong, God!"

I began to pray inwardly, "Jesus, I want my heart to be right." Finally, after several minutes, I felt able to lay my thoughts and feelings bare before Him. My face was still pressed against the floor as I prayed, "Heavenly Father, I repent of my anger and my disappointment. I choose to count myself dead to sin. I give myself completely to Jesus and to all that He accomplished on the Cross for me. Please forgive me. I surrender Florida to you; the house and my dreams. Give me strength to help George and not to hinder him.

"And above all," I prayed, "help me to follow you."

A familiar scene popped into my mind. For months now, George and I had prayed by the side of our bed,

"God, don't let us waste our lives." Was this the answer? Was moving to Tennessee actually part of God's plan?

• • •

THINGS MOVED QUICKLY after that. The very next day, George handed in his notice, much to the surprise of Dr. Teigland, who spent the next three months trying his hardest to keep him. He even flew George to the Bahamas to treat a prize bull, in a desperate bid to persuade him to stay in south Florida. But it was all to no avail. Once he had made up his mind, George Jackson was not one to look back. Our house went on the market and sold immediately.

The deal was done. There was no turning back.

So as spring edged closer to summer, we began, once again, to pack up our lives, resolving to spend as much time with the Bible study as we could. We were living in the midst of a spiritual revival. But we also knew that we would soon be moving on. It wasn't unusual for us to be out two or three evenings a week as our time drew to a close. So that's how we found ourselves back at the Fort Lauderdale Sheraton in May 1967, doing our best to cram in all the teaching that we could in the few weeks that remained; hungry for God, with no idea of what lay ahead. And that's when we first met Derek Prince.

It was a familiar scene by now and one that we had

experienced more than a dozen times before: the crowded room, the low ceiling lights, and the neatly laid-out rows of soft-backed chairs.

But tonight was different. Derek was different.

He was a well-dressed Englishman in his early fifties, over six feet tall with thinning black hair. His crisp white shirt and flecked tie were visible beneath the fashionably wide lapels of his buttoned plaid suit. But it was the weight of his résumé that set him apart: a fellow of Kings College, Cambridge, he was one of the foremost scholars of his generation, a philosopher who had studied under the great Ludwig Wittgenstein. Fluent in Latin and ancient Greek, Derek Prince had been an atheist who had started reading the Bible as a philosophical experiment. Yet, as he did so, sitting in an army barracks at the start of World War II, he had encountered Jesus for himself. Suddenly, he had realized that Christianity wasn't an academic system, but a relationship with a person.

Surely," I thought to myself, "he was as educated as Dr. Amos Boren. He must know about the ancient manuscripts and the different translations." Yet Derek Prince believed in the Baptism of the Holy Spirit and taught across the country, on those very verses from Mark 16 about "casting out demons" and "speaking in tongues." He wasn't, as Dr. Boren would argue, "a simpleton peddling emotional experience not rooted in scripture." He taught the Bible seriously, methodically, and with an authority I had never heard before and rarely have since.

And that night, he taught on baptism: not the Baptism of the Spirit, but baptism in water.

"John's baptism," Derek began, his elegant accent capturing the attention of those in the room, "was a 'baptism of repentance.' Scripture tells that he called the nation of Israel to the waters of the Jordan to repent of their sins and to 'prepare the way' for the coming Messiah. So why did Jesus, who had no sin, still come to John to be baptized? John himself questioned it. 'I need to be baptized by you,' he told Jesus, 'why are you coming to me?'

"Listen to Jesus' answer in Matthew, chapter 3: 'It is proper for us to do this to fulfill all righteousness.' People of God," Derek continued, "Jesus humbled himself and went down into the Jordan River, not to be cleansed from sin, but as an act of obedience to the Father. And when he did so, he modeled something for us, demonstrating that we also need to make a public, outward step to testify to the inner righteousness that He made available on the cross.

"Baptism doesn't cleanse you from sin. We do it so that we might openly identify with His burial and resurrection and show the world that we have died to our carnal nature. From then on, we choose to live a crucified life for Christ.

"Turn with me to Mark, chapter 16, verse 16." I glanced down the row to Sally, who sat wide-eyed and tearful. "Jesus put it simply like this: 'Whoever believes and is baptized will be saved.'

"God's way of salvation is still the same: first believe, then be baptized. This is the pattern of the early church: Peter preached on the Day of Pentecost and three thousand men were baptized that very day. In Acts, chapter 8, Philip had barely led the Ethiopian eunuch to the Lord when he stopped his chariot at a pool of water and said, 'Why shouldn't I be baptized?' The New Testament record shows that baptism normally followed conversion without delay.

"So my question to you tonight is the same. Here is water," he said, motioning toward the ocean. "What are you waiting for? Why shouldn't you also be baptized?"

There was no question in our minds that night as we sat in that ballroom on Fort Lauderdale beach: we needed to respond. The Bible commanded it, and we wanted to be obedient. Yes, George had been 'sprinkled' as a child in the Methodist church, more than once in fact, but he had been too young to believe.

"Let's meet tomorrow," Derek suggested in conclusion, before pointing out a slightly younger minister sitting in the front row. He was in his early forties, only ten years our senior, but his light brown beard was already clouding into grey. "Don Basham and I will be there at two o'clock on the beach in front of this hotel. Bring your bathing suits if you want to be baptized."

And with that, the meeting ended.

The next day was Sunday. I awoke early, thinking about the decision we had made the night before. I knew we had been challenged by the Holy Spirit to take another step toward the Lord. Besides, we were both excited to have this opportunity with our friends from the Bible study *before* we left Florida. It felt like a fresh beginning.

It was then that I heard the low murmur of voices drifting down the hall. It sounded as though George and Allen were up as well.

"So, *why* are you and mother getting baptized?" Allen was asking.

"It's because Jesus told us we needed to do it." George was explaining carefully. "He did it, and the Bible says that we should follow His example." He paused thoughtfully. "It's also a way we can show God that we want to live our lives in a way that is pleasing to Him."

There was a moment's silence before Allen spoke again. "May I join you, Daddy?"

• • •

THE WIND PICKED UP shortly after lunch. Most days, the calm turquoise water met the pale blue sky far off on the horizon. But on this particular Sunday afternoon, the powerful spring sunshine was weakened by a line of billowing clouds. The strengthening ocean swells reflected a hint of grey, and the large, swooping pelicans blended perfectly into their surroundings as they each, in turn, dove for fish in the sea.

About fifty of us stood together at the water's edge: a mismatched collage of black bathing suits, white t-shirts, and yellow swimming caps. Allen looked excited in his dark brown trunks, kicking spray at Phillip, who was shrieking playfully in response. Doyle was down on his knees, hands digging in the sand. Derek Prince stood there mingling with the crowd, his pale, thin legs and pristinely pressed shirt setting him apart from the young people who were gathering all around. I looked at George and smiled. What a picture!

A hush fell over the group as a man waded into the ocean, pressing through the waves. For a minute, there was silence, apart from the shrieking of seagulls and the rhythmic crash of the surf. Derek soon joined him, and they stood a little ways out in the water facing the shore, the waves rising and falling just below their knees. I shifted my position to get a clearer view, keeping a wary eye on Doyle as I did. I figured the other man must be Don Basham, the minister who had been introduced by Derek the night before.

"We're here today to make a public statement about our faith in God," Don Basham began.

"Those of you who are taking this step are doing so for three simple reasons," he said. "First, as Derek said last night, because Jesus commanded us to do so and you are seeking to obey His voice in your life. Second, to put to death your old man and be buried with Christ in the waters of baptism.

"And finally," he continued, as the wind whipped up the white surf behind him, "so that you can testify that you have been raised up with Him in 'newness of life.'"

Then he looked at all of us and asked, "Who's first?"

Neil held up his hand and stepped forward confidently, grinning from ear to ear. "I guess the Sunday school president should probably go first," he said, winking at Bud. He began to wade out boldly toward Derek and Don.

"Ex–Sunday school president!" chided Velma, as she followed close behind. The rest of us laughed.

George and I stayed back with the boys as others began wading out to wait their turn. A moment later, after moving out deeper, the three men turned together and faced the shore: Neil in the middle, flanked by Derek and Don.

"Based on your profession of faith in the Lord Jesus Christ, I baptize you in the Name of the Father, the Son, and the Holy Spirit," declared Derek as Neil momentarily vanished beneath the waves. A split second later he emerged, dripping triumphantly as a big cheer went up from the crowd.

Velma followed, then the Fellers, the cheers and clapping getting louder with every plunge. I looked around me, struck by the two worlds colliding. The Kingdom of God had come to Fort Lauderdale beach. And it was a sight to see: vacationers beneath umbrellas, reading their newspapers and pretending not to notice, and kids building sandcastles, stealing inquisitive glances at us as they did.

"I baptize you in the name of the Father, the Son, and the Holy Spirit!" The sound of those words was carried inland on the wind.

Soon, Velma came up to me, one towel draped around her waist, the other wrapped around her hair.

"It's your turn, Betty. I'll sit with the boys."

A moment later, the waves were up to my chest. I held my nose and closed my eyes expectantly.

"In the Name of the Father, the Son, and the Holy Sp—"

I was already underwater as Derek finished those words, and I was back on my feet in an instant, water cascading over my head. I took a moment to drink in the presence of God as the waves rose and fell around me—I was utterly amazed! There I was, standing in the shallows of a limitless ocean, and I felt like I had been washed with all the cleansing power of the sea.

Wiping the water from my eyes, I saw George patiently waiting his turn while Allen stood beside him looking on.

"Based on your profession of faith in the Lord Jesus Christ . . ."

George went down hard, back striking flat against the surface of the water. Derek and Don struggled to lift him, and it seemed like an eternity before he burst upright, arms crossed stiffly across his chest and eyes shut tight. There was a peace on his face that I had never seen before. He clasped Derek's hand in a firm handshake, then motioned for Allen to wade in deeper.

Within a minute, Allen, too, was gently held under and flicked effortlessly back out of the waves, like a buoy propelled upwards after being submerged. Over on the shore the crowd broke out in a hymn that kept gathering force as more of us joined in.

> *Oh, victory in Jesus,*
> *My savior forever*
> *He sought me*
> *And he bought me*
> *With his redeeming blood*
> *He loved me*
> *Ere I knew him*
> *And all my love is due him*
> *He plunged me to victory*
> *Beneath the cleansing flood*

On the Front Lawn, Ready for Church

At Home in North Miami Beach

Mary Booth
(Aunt Mary)

Hollywood Hills Home, 4811 Jackson Street

Allen and Phillip

Allen and Phillip Riding "Sue"

Phillip, Doyle and Allen, 1968 Murfreesboro

Allen, Phillip and Doyle, 1968

Doyle, Phillip & a Lamb

Veterinary Clinic

Dr. Jackson and Famous Stallion, Sun's Delight

Salem Road
Property,
Farm House

George and Betty, Beside the Clinic

George and Betty, with Sun's Delight

George and Betty, 1970

Allen, Doyle and Phillip

The Family

First Public Meeting Place, World Outreach Church

George Preaching, 1980

Apartment, Efrata Street, Jerusalem

Family Home & Veterinary Clinic

World Outreach Church, October, 1982

World Outreach Church Sanctuary 1984

World Outreach Church, 2013

Three Crosses Sanctuary, 2013

Front Row: Joan Judd, Nadine Feller, Bud Cobb, Dot Cobb, Betty Jackson, George Jackson and Dr. Marie Brink.
Back Row: Chuck Judd, Bob Feller, Dr. Neil Frank, Velma Frank, Bert Smith, Beth Smith, Johanna Brammer, John Brammer, Sharon Stitely, Sherry Taylor and Orville Brink.

Our faith took root while amongst this wonderful group of people. We want to especially thank Bud and Dot Cobb who taught us the great truths of the Bible, and opened their hearts and their home to us.

The original prayer group from Hollywood Hills, many of whom are mentioned in this book, gathered in Murfreesboro for a forty-five year reunion, celebrating the faithfulness of God in all of our lives. It was truly great being together again and catching up on children and grandchildren.

Scan this code with your camera-equipped smartphone to view the companion video for Chapter Seven. If you do not have the QR app on your phone, visit your app store and search for *QR code reader*.

EIGHT

RUMORS OF WAR

The Lord of hosts is with us;
the God of Jacob is our refuge.
Psalm 46:11

B ud's house was filled with people that Sunday night. George and I sat quietly in a makeshift row of folding chairs that were clustered together, legs interlocking, along the baseboards of the sunken living room wall.

I looked at the faces we had come to love: Sherry sitting next to me—close as a sister; I didn't know anyone who could make me laugh like she did. Bud—"nauseating," according to Sherry, because he gave us no option to stay the way we were. Then there was Dot, the perfect hostess, hovering in the entrance to welcome the latecomers as they pressed into the doorways, filling the last few empty chairs or eagerly finding a place to sit on the floor. There was an ache in the pit of my stomach as I caught Marie's steady smile, Velma's soft laugh, and the boom of Neil's voice from the other side of the room.

I had found such friends here; men and women who had changed our lives. I didn't think we would find their like in Tennessee.

"Jesus," I said to myself, recognizing a little quicker this time where my thoughts were taking me, "I choose to make my will obedient to Yours."

The chattering around us ceased as Bud stood up. I could see Derek Prince—our guest for the night—sitting to his right, with his wife Lydia beside him. She was some twenty-five years older than him, and her white hair and simple, elegant dress reminded me a little of George's grandmother. After a brief word of introduction, Bud sat down. Derek leaned forward in his chair, held up his Bible and began to pray: "Heavenly Father, take these scriptures and impress them on our hearts. May the words I speak be anointed by the Holy Spirit, that our lives would be changed forever. Amen." A hush fell upon the meeting as he opened his Bible and began to read:

> *And you will hear of wars and rumors of wars.*
> *See that you are not troubled; for all these*
> *things must come to pass, but the end is not yet.*
> (Matthew 24:6)

"Tonight," he began somberly, "we hear rumors of war." As he leaned forward in his chair, at the far end of that crowded living room, there was an earnestness in his face that seemed a little out of place in this affluent, easy-going suburb of Hollywood Hills.

"I'm not sure how many of you realize this," he continued, "but as dawn approaches in the Middle East, three Soviet-backed Arab armies are preparing to annihilate the reborn state of Israel. This very night, Syrian and Jordanian troops are mustering on her eastern borders and Egyptian president Gamal Nasser is publicly vowing to drive the Jewish people into the sea!"

I looked around—most of our friends' faces were as blank as mine. Though we were beginning to get used to Derek's accent and methodical style, there was something still quite foreign about his speech and demeanor; something a little intimidating. I had always been intrigued to hear about events in other nations, but it was hard to understand how talk of war in the Middle East affected me. I had a house to pack, three children to care for, and a husband gone from first light to dark.

And a week from now, we would be arriving in Tennessee!

Derek continued, seizing my full attention again. "These rumors are all the more significant when we realize that just thirty years ago Adolf Hitler was making similar threats against the Jews of Europe. Six million of them perished before the world woke up.

"Now for us here, in this beautiful home, surrounded by calm beaches and the gentle stirring of the ocean breeze, it's hard to grasp the fear that is gripping the hearts of the Jewish people re-gathered in Israel. They are a people who have returned to the land of their forefathers, after two thousand years of wandering, exactly as promised in the Scriptures. Yet they remain a hated people; facing implacable foes and improbable odds. That's why I want you to turn with me, this evening, to Matthew, chapter twenty-four. You see, Jesus is speaking to our world today:

> *Nation will rise against nation, and kingdom against kingdom. There will be famines and earthquakes in various places. All these are the beginning of birth pains.*
> (Matthew 24:7–8 NIV)

"Wars, conflicts, famines, and earthquakes." His words hung heavily in the air. "Jesus warned us that these are 'the beginning of birth pains.' So the question we need to ask ourselves tonight is this: what do these birth pains signify? What is about to be birthed in the earth?"

My eyes were fixed on the small New Testament in my lap, but my ears were tuned to that distinctive voice, so rich and commanding in the gathering twilight of early June. His air of authority was unmistakable: he handled the gilt-edged Bible in his hand with ease and confidence, unlocking its treasures word by word, accurately and precisely—without even needing to look down. In my heart,

I knew this was not just another Bible study in Bud and Dot's home. There was something supernatural in the atmosphere, as though the words of Jesus were reaching down through the centuries to me—to us—this particular night.

"We sometimes forget that Jesus was a prophet," Derek continued, his measured tones beginning to pick up speed. "The people of His time acknowledged Him as a prophet, even though they didn't acknowledge Him as the Son of God. In fact, He was the greatest of all the Hebrew prophets. Here we step into the narrative at a critical moment in His earthly ministry, just days before the crucifixion. It is His last opportunity to explain the things that are going to take place on earth immediately before His return, entrusting those closest to him to record His words for future generations like ours. 'Heaven and earth will pass away,' He tells them, in verse thirty-five, 'but My words will by no means pass away.'

"But for many Christians today," Derek challenged, "Jesus' words have passed away. They read the Bible as a historical document, a guide to ethics and a basis of religious observance. But they have no conviction that it is living and real. They don't believe that these words are speaking to our generation. So they don't listen."

He paused and looked out, with a penetrating gaze, over the heads of the forty or fifty men and women in the room. At that moment, I couldn't help feeling he was speaking directly to me. I glanced at George, diligently scribbling in his notebook. Did he feel that way, too?

"The sorrows Jesus speaks of," Derek explained, after taking a small sip of water, "are nothing less than the contractions that precede his Second Coming and the birthing of His Kingdom on earth. 'What will be the sign of Your coming?' the disciples ask in the third verse. And the picture that Jesus paints, as He begins to answer their question, is one of childbirth and travail: a time of trouble, of confusion, and of conflict—but a time of purpose. For, my friends, you can be sure, He is coming back!

"So when we look at the Middle East tonight, as the surrounding armies converge like a noose around Israel's neck, Jesus reminds us not to fear. Something of immense prophetic significance may be taking place in the world, but there is still one final act of history left to come.

"Because of all the signs Jesus speaks of in Matthew twenty-four," he continued, without hesitation, "none is the sign of His coming. All of these troubles are part of the birth pains, the context on earth, in which he steps back onto the stage of human history. 'But the end is not yet.'

"So what, then, will be 'the sign of His coming of the end of the age'? He singles it out in verse fourteen:

> *And this gospel of the kingdom will be preached in the whole world as a testimony to all nations, and then the end will come.* (Matthew 24:14 NIV)

"The real initiative in world history, then, is not with the politicians, not with the military commanders, not with the scientists, but with the Church. Because the Church is the only group of people that can bring about the closing sign of the age: the proclamation of this gospel of the kingdom. It does not depend on President Nasser of Egypt or King Hussein of Jordan. The end of these things depends on you, and on me, laying down our lives to ensure that the gospel is preached to all nations.

"So what are you living for? Are you living for an easy life, a better job, higher pay, a larger house, a better car? Or are you living for this purpose, that this gospel of the kingdom may be proclaimed in all the world as a witness to all the nations?"

There was a period of uncomfortable silence. I felt Sherry tap my shoulder and I turned my head. "Well, he's sure rocking the boat," she said in a loud whisper. George glanced toward us both as Derek began to read again:

Now learn this lesson from the fig tree: As soon as its twigs get tender and its leaves come out, you know that summer is near. Even so, when you see all these things, you know that it is near, right at the door. I tell you the truth, this generation will certainly not pass away until all these things have happened. Heaven and earth will pass away, but my words will never pass away. (Matthew 24:32–35 NIV1984)

"My friends," he pleaded, "if we ever needed to learn the parable of the fig tree, it is now. The fig tree is Israel. And despite the centuries of exile and persecution, Jesus promises at the 'end of the ages,' that she will once again put forth her leaves and become a nation again.

"We were there when it happened in 1948," he added, stealing a knowing glance at his wife, Lydia. "Nothing like this has ever been seen on earth. God brought His people home from the four corners of the Earth, according to His Word. And I assure you tonight, *He will not* let this people be removed from the earth or pushed into the sea—no matter the odds against them!

"There's a reason I can say that with such confidence. The key lies in the word generation, a richer word in Greek than in English. He's not just talking about those living in the same period of history. He is speaking of the Jewish people in all their generations. This people, Jesus assures us, will endure until His return.

"So tonight, as we hear of the rumors of war, we need to look up. God is Israel's refuge, as the Psalmist says, 'He will help her at the break of dawn.'

"But what about us?" He paused momentarily. "To-night we have a choice: to be bystanders in the work of God or to participate with Him. We may be far removed from the theater of this conflict, but Scripture commands us to stand as 'watchmen' on the walls of Jerusalem and to 'give Him no rest' till 'He makes Jerusalem a praise in the earth.' The very words of Jesus demand that we respond. His call is simple: to lay down our lives for the gospel and to 'pray for the peace of Jerusalem.' Are you willing?"

With these words, Derek folded his hands and leaned back in his chair. There was silence as the weight of conviction fell on the room. For several moments, no one moved. Dot stood first and moved quietly toward the kitchen, giving Bud his cue to thank Derek and Lydia on our behalf. "You have given us so much to think about," he ventured.

"Scratch that," Sherry whispered in my ear, "He didn't just rock the boat, he drained the lake!"

George slowly closed his notebook and stood up without saying a word. I followed him reluctantly, not wanting the moment to end, as we filed into the kitchen for some refreshments. Nobody was talking much at first. These were sobering words. We were being faced with a choice to go forward or to walk away.

Before long, Sherry found me again. The room was livening up a little as she leaned close and said in her slow Georgian drawl, "Bet he doesn't even sweat the price of eggs." I laughed as I always did when she was around, but I knew that she, too, was challenged by Derek. He had left his home and nation to live in Israel, Africa, and across North America; the cost of daily bread did not seem to concern him.

"Trouble is," Sherry remarked, "I don't think you can

ever take one day off after a message like this. There isn't even a day when you can take the time to pitch a fit."

I reached over and squeezed her hand. "There's not much incentive to go back," I replied. Although it had been a couple of years since I had battled with cancer, I knew what it was like to feel the despair and hopelessness of life without Jesus. I also knew the joy of getting to know Him! No matter *where* He led, I wanted to follow and I knew Sherry did too.

I caught George's eye as he was chatting with Bud in the entrance to the living room, and I could see him beginning to move toward me. I was curious to hear his thoughts, but I knew I might have to wait a while. He would share with me eventually—when he was ready.

"Is this woman bothering you?" George said to Sherry, with a grin, as he grabbed hold of my arm. It was time to go. I took a deep breath and started to say good-bye. Sherry waved me on. "We'll all be there to see you off!" she assured me. "I'm not saying good-bye right now!"

We were both quiet as we stepped out into the Florida night. Walking along the wide sidewalks, I reviewed Derek's message in my mind: the rumors of war, the challenge of the gospel, the call to prayer. I didn't fully understand why this night was so important—it just was. Derek understood so much more about the Bible than we did, and I wanted to know more of what he knew.

Soon, George's long strides got the better of me. I

looked up and saw him several paces ahead of me. Normally, I would run and catch up with him, but I wanted to savor the scene in front of me one last time. The waning crescent moon was rising low over the city skyline, the stars twinkled in the clear, dark blue sky. The royal poincianas had burst out in all their colors, just in time for one last final goodbye, and the bright orange blossoms massed to form a canopy over the sidewalk. I remembered the night I had decided to paint them on my kitchen wall—I was so happy here.

A few minutes later, we came to our house—my dream home, surrounded by fruit trees and flowers. The white brick shone in the moonlight. Four stately royal palms shot high up into the sky, their tips seeming to touch the stars.

I began to sing softly:

He touched me, Oh He touched me,
And oh the joy that floods my soul!
Something happened and now I know,
He touched me and made me whole.

George finally glanced behind him. In moments like these, he knew that when I started singing, I was trying my best not to cry. I managed a half-hearted smile, wondering whether he could even see it in the dark.

I guess he did, because he stopped, turned back and

pulled me close. I put my head on his chest and he wrapped his arms around me.

"I'll miss the mornings," he conceded, meeting my emotion with a little of his own, "when it's warm and balmy and still almost dark. I'll miss eating breakfast at the restaurant by the racetracks and meeting the other vets between the barns: all the other nobodies like me!"

I was grateful there was something he was going to miss and that he was starting to talk. We began to walk side by side again.

"Betty Joyce," he said, after a moment, and I knew then that these weren't the deep things in his heart. It was what he shared next. "How do you go to church all your life and miss the relationship between the Bible and everyday life?" He spoke in such an earnest, wistful voice. "I have read the Bible in the past," he continued, "people, places, history, and facts—but never like Derek. He talks about it like a road map, yet I don't even know it well enough to read the signs."

George stopped to unlock our front door, then turned around to look at me. "We have to learn more!" he said. I could feel his passion as he grabbed my hand, closed his eyes, and prayed a prayer I had never heard him speak before. "God, we pray tonight for the peace of Jerusalem. Defend your people, Israel. Protect them from their enemies. And let your kingdom come on earth as it is in heaven. Use us and our children, in the name of Jesus, Amen."

What came next was like the fresh Florida breeze, and I felt a shiver of excitement. It was the tangible presence of the Holy Spirit, which we had only begun to recognize over the past few months. We stood there for a moment, on the doorstep, before stepping into the house.

• • •

THE SUN WAS OUT in full strength the next morning. It was Monday the fifth of June and our final week in Florida had begun. George was long gone to the race-tracks, and Allen was eating breakfast at the kitchen table. Doyle and Phillip, meanwhile, were moving through the empty house dressed as Batman and Robin, wearing costumes I thought I had packed several days before, trying unsuccessfully to convince their older brother to join in.

I was wiping finger-marks off the glass patio doors, highlighted by the bright morning sun, when suddenly, out of the corner of my eye, I happened to see one of my Jewish neighbors rush into our yard. There were no fences in our subdivision and the lots naturally joined together. I paused, with my cloth held in mid-air to watch him. Mr. Straus was normally a quiet man—a gifted artist and furniture designer by trade—but now he was waving his arms every which way and yelling, followed closely by his wife, who was equally distraught.

"What in the world are they doing?" I thought.

Curious, I opened the door and looked to my right. Now another Jewish neighbor was also heading into my yard, in tears, with her children sobbing behind her! I had no idea what was going on.

I rushed outside to join them, "What's wrong?!" I asked, as they all turned toward me. I looked back and forth between them, my own heart becoming more and more unsettled the longer I looked. Mr. Straus's eyes were bloodshot, and I noticed his wife's fingernails bitten down to the flesh.

"Haven't you heard?!" they asked, incredulously.

"Heard *what?*" I said, checking toward the house to see if the boys had followed me out. They had. A short distance away, Allen, Phillip, and Doyle stood, listening intently.

"Israel's at war!" My other neighbor wailed, and everyone began to talk at once. "The Arabs have attacked," said one. "Our cousins have left their children in their beds and gone to war!" said another. "We have emptied our bank accounts to help," Mrs. Straus chimed in. "There is nothing left to give."

I stared at them, astounded, remembering the scripture that Derek had quoted from Psalm forty-six the night before: "God is in the midst of her, she shall not be moved; God shall help her, just at the break of dawn."

I said the first thing that came to my mind. I wanted so much to give them some word of encouragement or hope. "Israel's going to win the war!" I said loudly, so they would hear me over the commotion. They stopped short and I felt all eyes turn on me. Now it was their turn to act shocked.

"There is a man George and I heard speak last night, and he said Israel would win the war," I explained.

The next few moments seemed endless—I had plenty to think about. This meant so much to them and so little to me, until now. Why?

The phone rang inside the house. Nobody moved. Allen took one look at me, then ran to answer it. "Mother! Sherry's on the phone," he called out a few seconds later.

"Betty!" She didn't even wait for me to reply. "Bob and I are standing in the kitchen right now, looking at a map of Israel. It is such a tiny country, surrounded on every side. Bob said common sense says they can't possibly win this war!"

But much to our surprise, they did.

Over the next few days, Israeli troops had liberated the Old City of Jerusalem from Jordanian occupation, bringing the entire city under Jewish sovereignty for the first time in more than two thousand years. In six days, the war was won, with the Sinai desert, the Golan Heights, Judea, Samaria, and Gaza all falling under Israeli control. A battle for survival had turned into a territorial triumph. It was the hand of God! There was no other explanation. Later, we would gain a much greater understanding of the significance of this moment. But that day, we knew all we needed to know. Scripture and life had converged to leave an unforgettable imprint on us.

I searched a few packed boxes for my stack of thank-you cards, and quickly wrote a note to Derek and Lydia Prince. Tennessee was halfway between Chicago, where they lived, and Florida, where they were spending more and more time ministering these days. Perhaps we would have the privilege of meeting them again.

June 5, 1967

Dear Brother Prince,

We want to thank you for your willingness to include us in the group that you baptized in the ocean at Fort Lauderdale earlier this month and for the Bible teaching we received at the home of Bud and Dot Cobb.

We have enclosed a small check to express our appreciation.

If you and Mrs. Prince are ever passing through Tennessee, we would be honored to have you stop and spend the night.

Sincerely,

George and Betty Jackson

Scan this code with your camera-equipped
smartphone to view the companion video
for Chapter Eight. If you do not have the QR
app on your phone, visit your app store and
search for *QR code reader.*

NINE

HAPPY ANNIVERSARY

*For this reason I kneel before the Father,
from whom every family in heaven and
on earth derives its name.*
Ephesians 3:14-15 (NIV)

I sat in the backseat between Doyle and Phillip, with books and ideas to entertain a two- and a five-year-old as we made the nine-hundred-mile journey from Miami to Murfreesboro.

Hour after hour the landscape changed. I sang softly to myself . . . singing to keep from crying.

> *O Lord my God! When I in awesome wonder*
> *Consider all the worlds Thy hands have made.*
> *I see the stars, I hear the rolling thunder,*
> *Thy power throughout the universe displayed.*

The words of the song washed over my heart. It was a new chapter in our lives. Today was our anniversary, Saturday, June 10, 1967: eleven years to the day since we had walked down the aisle and vowed to spend the rest of our lives together. I thought back to our wedding on that bright afternoon in Sarcoxie, Missouri, light streaming through the stained glass window behind the altar. It was the famous picture of Jesus knocking at the door. How little we knew about Him then. What would the next eleven years hold, I wondered?

"Are we stopping for lunch?" Allen asked.

"We have a surprise lunch for you," I said, reaching for the cooler. "Daddy and I are fasting today."

During our final months in Florida, we had gotten into a routine of fasting and praying for our nation once a week. It was a season of great turmoil in America, between Vietnam and the Civil Rights movement.

Somewhere past Atlanta, Doyle woke up. Gone were the flat swamp plains of north-central Florida with their bayous, sycamores, and cypress groves, and we found our car climbing through thick wooded hills filled with towering pines, beech trees, and oaks. The farther we drove, the larger the trees seemed to become, with their twisted vines of ivy winding up wide trunks like veins.

As Lookout Mountain came into view I heard myself singing again:

> *When through the woods and forest glades I wander*
> *And hear the birds sing sweetly in the trees;*
> *When I look down from lofty mountain grandeur*

And hear the brook and feel the gentle breeze:
Then sings my soul, my Saviour God, to Thee;
How great Thou art, how great Thou art!

Doyle suddenly noticed the tall trees, dressed in their leafy grandeur and swaying in the breeze, such as he had never seen in south Florida. He covered his little eyes with one hand, pointed for us to see. It was obvious he was frightened. While George and I felt compassion, both Allen and Phillip found it amusing. After explaining the change of scenery to a two-year-old the best we could and ensuring that Doyle was at peace again, we all enjoyed a good laugh.

"How much farther, Daddy?" Phillip exclaimed.

George replied, "Very soon we will be in the state of Tennessee, then two more hours and we should arrive at our new house."

I suggested we take time to pray together, and opened the prayer: "Heavenly Father, thank you that you have chosen Murfreesboro as a home for us."

"We ask that you would give wisdom and understanding to the leaders of our new city; that it would become a prosperous place. That we too would prosper in our business and in our spiritual lives," George continued.

"Thank you for bringing us to a place where we have the freedom to live out our faith and share it with others," I said, thinking back to Aunt Mary and her stories about the Christians in Cuba: of women watching their husbands die before a firing squad. We were so thankful to live in America.

"And I pray, Lord, give us a good pastor in Murfreesboro," George added, as we passed through Chattanooga, along the edge of the Tennessee river gorge, surrounded on both sides by the rising foothills of the great Appalachian mountain range. "God, I pray for a pastor who will teach the people Your Word . . ."

"And who would baptize the people in water," Allen volunteered.

George caught my eye in the mirror and grinned. Sometimes, children learned best by imitation.

"Amen!" George said, closing our prayer time.

And so our time of prayer ended as naturally as it began.

By now the royal palms and balmy breezes of Florida were half a world away, as our station wagon slowly climbed the steep, winding inclines that crossed the ancient land barrier between America's eastern seaboard and her central plains. To our left was a sheer face of sliced rock, with trickles of water tumbling down in makeshift waterfalls by the side of the road. Finally, as we crested the peak of Monteagle, the gently rolling hills of the Tennessee Valley came into view, with corn, hay fields and large herds of beef cattle dotting the landscape. Soon, the ground began to level out. The central divider filled with long grass, purple thistles, and endless patches of Queen Anne's lace. Instead of the coastal palmetto sand, I saw red dirt peeking through the grass.

It had just rained. The road was steaming from the heat of the day. Thick humidity hung in the air. Barns flanked the highway on either side.

"Look!" Allen said. "That barn is falling down!" Behind a small farmhouse stood a red, dilapidated barn. Large, white block letters stood out against a black roof: WHEN YOU SEE ROCK CITY YOU'VE SEEN THE BEST.

"There's another one!" Phillip noticed, turning his neck to stare at another advertisement.

Soon it became a game of who could spot the barn and read the slogan first: BEAUTIFUL BEYOND BELIEF. EIGHTH WONDER OF THE WORLD. BRING YOUR CAMERA.

"Mother!" I followed Phillip's gaze. "What does that one say?"

I read the clear, bold letters. MILLIONS HAVE SEEN ROCK CITY—HAVE YOU?

"Dad, what in the world is Rock City?" Allen inquired, bewildered.

"We just passed it, Allen," George replied, "about half an hour ago, on top of those hills outside Chattanooga. It's a—"

"See Rock City! See Rock City!" Phillip and Allen chanted quietly together.

"We have left beaches and palm trees and swimming

pools for Rock City," I thought.

It was late afternoon by the time we pulled off Highway 41. We drove across town to our new home in Scotland Acres, around the historic courthouse square, out East Main toward the university campus. We arrived at the modest, yellow brick, ranch-style house with a solitary bush on the front lawn, bought during a whirlwind two-day visit at the end of May. It was a new and pleasant neighborhood.

There was a man sitting on the front porch steps when we arrived, his thin, graying hair obscured by a cream trilby hat with a thick black band above the narrow rim. He looked up as we approached the driveway and took one last puff of the filterless Lucky Strike that was dangling from his hand. He then got to his feet with a stretch, flicked the finished cigarette onto the ground, and extinguished it with a swift twist of his left heel.

"Vance, good to see you. Have you been here long?" George called out as the two men walked toward each other and warmly shook hands.

"No," he said, glancing at his watch. "About two minutes or so. You said you would try and get here by four, and I know you pretty well, George."

It was Vance Paschal, a local horse trader with whom George had formed a friendship on some of his previous trips to the area. He was a thin man who always wore short sleeves and blue khaki pants and who specialized in palomino horses. In fact, he knew just about every palomino within a radius of a hundred miles: who owned them, where they were stabled, and their blood lines. Vance and his wife, E.E., were two of the few people we knew in Murfreesboro at the time, and we were sure glad to see him.

"Now let me take Doyle out to the farm," Vance continued. "It'll give you guys some time to get settled in. Then E.E.'s invited you for dinner. Hope you're all hungry, she's outdone herself this time!"

With that, he scooped Doyle up onto his shoulders and set off for his truck.

I was thankful not to have a toddler underfoot as we started unloading boxes in the hallway, knowing we needed to make the most of the daylight while we had it. After an hour and a half, we called it a day and headed out along Halls Hill Pike to the Paschals' farm. They lived in a rock veneer farmhouse. Across the road was their red painted pole barn. Vance sat in the shadow of the largest maple tree I had ever seen. There were two white rocking chairs on their front porch, and on a small porch near the back door of the house sat a dozen cases of Coca-Cola bottles, unopened and neatly stacked to one side.

"Have yourself a Coke and some peanuts 'til dinner's ready!" Vance told the boys as soon as we arrived. Phillip glanced at me and his look said it all: this must be the wealthiest family in all of Tennessee—they have hundreds of Cokes!

Vance and George stayed outside talking, with their arms folded, while I went in search of Doyle. I passed through the living room, where I noticed the large family Bible lying open on a beautiful marble top table and a sewing machine tucked away in the corner. As I made my way into the kitchen, I saw lighted cabinets with glass doors filled with R. S. Prussia porcelain, produced by Reinhold Schlegelmilch at his factory in the town that is now Suhl, Germany, from the late 1800s through the beginning of World War I.

Doyle and E.E. were in the kitchen. She had settled him at the breakfast table, where he was munching on cornbread, the best I had ever tasted. Her own children were all grown and had left home, and she seemed delighted to have found a blonde-haired two-year-old to spoil as her own, along with her grandson, Mac Allen, who lived with his parents nearby.

I was deeply grateful.

As we sat down to our dinner, I looked around the table. It was our first day in Murfreesboro, and we had received the warmest welcome we could have ever imagined.

• • •

GEORGE HAD VISITED horse barns in the Middle Tennessee area and had been invited by a local veterinarian to do some reproductive exams while on our past visits to Tennessee.

This was our first week in Murfreesboro, and we were adjusting to a new schedule. George, dressed in his khakis and jodhpur boots, had gone out to organize the station wagon. He began making a list of medications and equipment we would be giving to the visiting pharmaceutical salesmen who would be dropping by.

When he finished breakfast, George left to go by some local stables as he was used to doing at the Florida practice. The morning was filled, as each stable had some brood mare work or a horse going short in his stride. George was trying to make himself a place in the horse culture of Middle Tennessee.

"Help us build this business in a way that honors you," we would pray as we knelt beside our bed together at night. One particular reading was from Psalm 90. "Lord, give us your favor! Establish the work of our hands for us; yes, establish the work of our hands."

A few days later, Vance stopped by. "Let me introduce you to some of the area trainers," he offered. "I am well acquainted with some of the owners and trainers in the barns."

George understood. Vance was right; the horse world had its own system of recommendation and referral. With Vance's help and a bit of persistence, one of the stables agreed to give him an opportunity—and George's practice began. Vance, indeed, was the answer to our prayers.

• • •

GEORGE'S DREAM WAS to build a clinic on a few acres of pastureland, with trees, a barn, and a creek. It needed to be accessible to the communities around us, so that horses could be easily brought in for treatment, with enough room to build a house of our own. We decided to set aside Tuesdays, every week, as a day to fast and pray, not just for our nation but for the right piece of land.

This Tuesday, George entered the kitchen area with something obviously on his mind.

"Betty, I need you to write a letter to Dr. Teigland," he announced.

Dr. Teigland? I waited.

"As I was driving home, something came to mind. When we left Florida, I took one of Teigland's sterilizing trays with me," George explained, a seriousness in his face. "It was from an old storeroom, and no one was using it. I didn't think he'd miss it. But I stole it, Betty. I know that God can't fully bless our business if I steal from someone else. I want to explain to him in a letter exactly what I did, to ask his forgiveness, and to send him a check to cover the value of the tray. I have looked it up in an equipment catalog and I know the amount I need to send him."

George dictated the letter while I typed it. He wrote

and signed a check, and I mailed it the very next day.

A few days later he followed up on it, asking me, "You sent the letter, didn't you?"

"Yes, George."

"Did you get a reply?"

"Not yet."

"Did the check get cashed?"

It was in the amount of thirty-five dollars, but that wasn't the point: the principle mattered more to George than the money. He wanted to make sure Dr. Teigland received restitution.

The whole incident made me think about my own life. The next thing I knew, I was convicted by the Holy Spirit! When I was ten years old growing up in Missouri, we lived out in the country near a Christian couple who had a worldwide radio ministry and a well-known peach orchard. I used to walk through the trees and pick a peach and eat it; I loved the fresh fruit. But God showed me that I had stolen them. So I, too, sent a letter—telling the couple what I had done and asking forgiveness. We had learned, for us, the importance of going forward required cleaning up the past.

Soon after, George got his first big stable. It was at Vic Thompson's barn, a large horse farm on Highway 41, west of Shelbyville, and it came, in part, because of his reputation for being trustworthy—particularly when it came to purchasing horses. One day, Vic Thompson called him to examine a beautiful show gelding that he had agreed to sell for twenty-five thousand dollars. George did the usual exam: he took blood samples, he observed the horse being ridden, then he performed a physical examination.

"Mr. Thompson," George said, calling his client away to one side. "This gelding is in fine condition—strong lungs, good heart. He looks perfect from the outside. But you probably don't realize he is blind in one eye. Only as I examined the back of the eye was it clear, the eye was nonfunctional." Vic reduced the price to fifteen thousand dollars, and the horse sold that day.

Within weeks, it seemed, our whole life changed. George's practice took over our small suburban home. One minute I was "Mother," and the next minute I was answering the phone, "Jackson Veterinary Office, may I help you?" George would occasionally bring home a sta-blehand's sick dog, and he was always willing to do what he could to help those who were unable to afford veter-inary care. One evening he even brought home a blind lamb. The bookshelves in the older boys' room were filled with drug supplies, while a certain section of the refrigera-tor was neatly stacked with laboratory samples.

I still remember the time a local drapery shop had completed an order for the sliding glass door in the kitchen. A nice man arrived to install the drapes, and was balanced on a step ladder, hammer in hand, when suddenly five-year-old Phillip burst into the room, opened the refrigerator, and called out: "Mother, what happened to all that horse manure that was in the refrigerator?"

I glanced toward the man on the ladder and noticed he never missed a lick with his hammer. The samples had been picked up by the laboratory. I often wondered what that man may have thought, but what could one say at such a time?

• • •

WE HADN'T BEEN in the house in Scotland Acres very long, yet we realized that the revival we had encountered in Florida had now begun to penetrate Middle Tennessee. Of all the adjustments in our lives, we knew that finding a church would probably be the most important.

It wasn't that there weren't any to choose from. Murfreesboro had a long list of well-established congregations nestled along the tree-lined streets, close to the public square: First Baptist Church, the original home of the State Baptist Convention; First Methodist; First Presbyterian; St. Paul's Episcopal Church; and Main Street Church of Christ. A few blocks away were St. Rose Catholic Church and an Assembly of God.

On the edge of Murfreesboro at that time was The Sword of the Lord, established by the internationally known Dr. John R. Rice. Only a few miles in the country was the Bill Rice Ranch, established by one of John Rice's brothers. The Ranch became a great place where both hearing and hearing-impaired children from across the nation could come to the countryside, ride horses, swim, enjoy cookouts, and experience a week of listening to the Gospel message.

We chose a church not far from our house, St. Mark's Methodist Church, located on East Main Street. Rev. Bill Moss was an amiable man who had a heart for the Lord; he warmly welcomed us. We appreciated Brother Moss so much, yet we yearned for the friends, the Bible study, and the teaching we had received in Florida.

That's when an encouraging note arrived unexpectedly in the mail.

> Dear Mr. and Mrs. Jackson,
>
> Thank you for your recent note and the gift to our ministry.
>
> I am writing to let you know that Lydia and I are intending to drive through Murfreesboro in the middle of August en route to Maryville, Tennessee. I have been invited to join several other men who will be speaking at a Christian gathering on the college campus there.
>
> If you would like, you may invite some friends into your home, and we could have a Bible lesson.
>
> In His Service,
> Derek Prince

"Maybe Derek could speak at our church!" George suggested excitedly, as we both read his note again. It had been two months since we arrived in Murfreesboro, and the thought of a Bible study was more than exciting. The next day George met with Brother Moss and asked if he would like to have Derek at the church for the Wednesday night meeting.

"Of course," he said, cheerfully. "I would be very interested to hear what he has to say."

• • •

IT WAS THE HEIGHT of summer. The midweek meeting was always held in the small chapel. A little more than a hundred people were gathered in the comfortable meeting place. George and I were sitting behind Derek and Brother Moss, next to Lydia. We hadn't been here long: we only knew a few people from the congregation, and we had no idea how such a prominent voice from within the emerging charismatic renewal would be received by the congregation at St. Mark's.

Brother Moss delivered a few words of introduction—Derek Prince was born in India of British parents; he was educated as a scholar of Greek and Latin at Eton College and Cambridge University, England, where he held a fellowship in ancient and modern philosophy at King's

College; he had grown up in the Church of England. Then Derek, who towered over the pews from the pulpit at the front of the chapel, began to speak.

"Upon entering the British Army in World War II, I could only take one book with me to the barracks. I had read books on Hinduism, Confucianism, Atheism. Yet there was one book of philosophy that I had never studied for myself. In searching for the one book that I could take, I chose the book that contained in it sixty-six books, the book of philosophy that I had never read: the Bible.

"I began in Genesis, at the beginning, just like any book one would read. I quickly realized that this book was unlike any piece of literature I had ever picked up in my life. It contained profound wisdom, but it wasn't mere philosophy; historical fact, but it was more than history. I couldn't place it, couldn't categorize it in any meaningful way. The more I read, the more convicted I became. How could I dismiss it; what if it were true?

"Slowly but surely, I found myself drawn by God's grace. I was invited to a small seaside church in the north of England, a far cry from the great cathedrals and chapels I had attended as a boy. The people were common, uneducated folk, but they had a peace in their lives that drew me in further. And the more I saw of them, the more I became aware of my own misery, until one evening, quite late, I determined to sit by my barrack room window and pray until something happened.

"I realized that I had no idea how to pray. I did not know to whom I should pray or what I should say. I could not even begin. I suppose I sat there on that stool for an hour or more as darkness descended, trying to pray, totally baffled.

"Then something happened that I find hard to explain. Just when I was ready to give up, I became aware of a presence: a power filling the room. And it was as though, through the power, there was a person standing before me. I did not know who He was, but I knew He had the answer. Words began to come out of my mouth; words that came from deep inside, "Unless you bless me, I will not let you go! I will not let you go! I will not let you go!" As I said those words, over and over again, something broke loose in the innermost part of my being. It was as though there had been a release, like a knot that had been tied there for many years had been undone. I began to weep like a child."

All around me there was silence. I waited eagerly to hear what Derek would say next. He continued.

"I had no idea why I was sobbing. I had no consciousness in my mind of anything about which I needed to cry, but still the tears flowed out of me. That was strange enough, but after about an hour of this, the tears began to change to laughter. Again, I had no conscious reason to be laughing; laughter was just flowing out through me. I kept on praying and crying and laughing into the night, my hands raised above my head.

"It wasn't until a few weeks later that I began to understand what had taken place that night; I had encountered the person of Jesus through the power of the Holy Spirit. I sought out the Christians I had met in that little church, and they opened up the pages of Scripture. My life started changing, as did my habits, my speech, and my desires. Then one night, they prayed for me to be baptized in the Holy Spirit. And as I stood there in their living room, I felt that same presence that had first come upon me in the barracks that night, and I began to speak in tongues, just as Jesus promised his disciples."

Again, I stole a quick glance around me. I had no doubt that Derek had spoken to the people of St. Mark's what they needed to hear. At the same time, I felt fearful that they might not believe his words.

"In that way I came to know that Truth is a Person. I had always been looking for an abstraction, a theory. I had been looking for an explanation but had found a Person. Without any process of reasoning, I knew that that person was Jesus of Nazareth. And that same power—the power of the Holy Spirit that changed my life—is here tonight if you are willing to receive."

Brother Moss got up and closed the meeting; yet again, his warmth shone through. He invited those present to come forward and ask questions. Derek stayed up front answering questions with George, while Lydia and I took the boys back to our house.

We drove the short distance in silence. It was good to hear Derek speak again, but I was still wondering how his message would be received.

"You were afraid when Derek mentioned the Holy Spirit Baptism," Lydia stated in her thick Danish accent. Not for one minute did I doubt what Lydia said to me was true. Neither did I want to deny it. Suddenly, I remembered the words of Jesus from Matthew 10:32–33:

> *Therefore whoever confesses Me before men, him I will also confess before My Father who is in heaven. But whoever denies Me before men, him I will also deny before My Father in heaven.*

"What you have said is true, Lydia. I don't want to feel that way ever again."

Lydia prayed for me in a thick torrent of Danish words. I had no idea what she was saying, but by the time she was finished, I felt sure I would never want to deny the Lord again.

When we arrived back at the house, I went to the kitchen and started making dinner while Lydia entertained Doyle.

In her young life, Lydia had set out on a courageous quest to know God's will for her life. In her search for God and her life's purpose, she was led to Jerusalem where she rescued scores of abandoned sick and orphaned children from disease and death. She clearly demonstrated a love for our boys.

George excitedly told us over dinner that Brother Moss had scheduled a three-day revival meeting the following March, inviting Derek to come back and minister to the entire congregation. We were amazed at the doors that had already opened so quickly in this community, and we visited with our guests late into the night.

I couldn't wait until spring.

Scan this code with your camera-equipped smartphone to view the companion video for Chapter Nine. If you do not have the QR app on your phone, visit your app store and search for **QR code reader.**

TEN

FERTILE GROUND

...For we are God's fellow workers;
you are God's field, God's building.
1 Corinthians 3:9 (NIV1984)

We both liked the property. It was a few acres off Halls Hill Pike—probably the sixth or seventh piece of land we'd seen. "I'm impressed," George said as we sat in the station wagon, trying to figure out where to build the clinic, a barn, and eventually a home.

"It's got everything we need, hasn't it George?" I asked, quietly hoping that perhaps our search might be over.

"It does," he said thoughtfully, before reaching forward to turn the key in the ignition. "But I'm just not sure it's the right one."

George put the car in reverse and began to back out.

"Would you like to come with me on my next call, or shall I drop you at home?"

"Where is it?"

"Out toward Lebanon."

"Sure. It's a beautiful day. It'll be nice to get out of town."

Allen and Phillip were in school, Doyle was fast asleep in the back seat, and I loved getting out of the house to see the Tennessee countryside with George, especially in the fall.

"I brought some crackers and cheese in case we ran past lunch."

"We will, Betty," George grinned, "no question of that!"

We watched the scenery fly by: rolling hills, turning leaves, and cattle dotted across grassy fields. This part of the world was growing on me.

"George, with all our hearts, I want God to do here what he did in Florida." I said all of a sudden after a long period of silence. "I want Him to move in this community!"

"I do too, Betty," George replied quietly.

But neither of us had any idea *how* He was going to accomplish it.

I reached into the glove compartment, pulled out my New Testament, and opened it. "George, where was that verse you were reading a few nights ago?"

"Somewhere in the middle of Romans, I think."

I thumbed through the Bible, scanning the pages for a verse George had pointed out a couple of days earlier, while we lay in bed reading the Bible together.

He quickly glanced over and pointed to the top of the

page. "Over there, I think."

"Is this it?" I started reading out loud:

> *Likewise the Spirit also helps in our weaknesses.*
> *For we do not know what we should pray for*
> *as we ought, but the Spirit Himself makes*
> *intercession for us with groanings which cannot*
> *be uttered.* (Romans 8:26)

"That sure is us," I agreed, letting out a huge sigh. "We're weak and we don't know what to pray! Let's do it right now."

George began a simple prayer asking for God's help. After all these months it was still an amazing experience to seek God together in this way. But it was a discipline to do so. We had to determine to put aside all the distractions that flooded our minds and simply do what the Scripture said, no matter how excited *or* discouraged we felt.

Five or ten minutes passed with us praying, George with his hands steady on the wheel, while I closed my eyes. Soon, a specific prayer began to form in my mind and I spoke it out. "Father, I pray for a man in Middle Tennessee who will take a stand for the Word of God and do what it says to do. A man who will teach the full truth of the gospel of Jesus. That . . ."

"We're here, Betty."

I looked up in surprise: a half hour had flown by!

George's clients were a wealthy couple who lived on a small hobby farm not far from Nashville, with several beautiful American saddle horses. George went with the owner to look at a chestnut mare in the far corner of the pasture while I laid out a blanket under a glorious spreading beech tree, set down our thermos of sweet tea, and opened up the crackers and cheese. Doyle immediately grabbed a cracker in each hand and started munching gleefully, taking alternate bites from the right and left hand, trying to figure out which he liked best.

After a few minutes of watching Doyle and admiring the farm, I saw the owner's wife walking toward us across the field. "May I get you something, Mrs. Jackson?" she asked, joining me in the shade.

"Thank you, but we have all we need," I said gratefully. "We even have some extra sweet tea here in the thermos. Would you like to join us?"

"I would, Mrs. Jackson. But I can't stay long."

"Please, call me Betty!"

She sat down on the blanket next to me with a smile and immediately started asking questions: what we thought of Murfreesboro and whether we missed Florida. She seemed genuinely drawn to something. Before I knew it, I was telling her my story, from the hopelessness of cancer to being baptized in the ocean. I didn't hold back. After a few minutes, she stared at me intently with a strange look in her eyes.

"You have almost convinced me to become a Christian," she said with a sad but proud smile. Then she stood up, brushed the grass off her pants, and headed back toward the house. I watched her go, feeling the ache of her inner turmoil.

"If only she had the courage to say yes," I thought. "How her life could be different!"

I had no idea how God was going to move in Middle Tennessee, in the lives of people like that well-to-do woman in the pasture. But now I was convinced even more: we needed Him. The fields were white for the harvest all around us—as white as the budding cotton in the fields. All I knew to do was pray.

> *Rejoice always, pray without ceasing, in*
> *everything give thanks; for this is the will*
> *of God in Christ Jesus for you.*
> (1 Thessalonians 5:16–18)

Every day, that verse would echo in my thoughts. What does it mean to "pray without ceasing"? Washing dishes, filing invoices, or scrubbing the floors, whenever I had the opportunity I would try to pray—sometimes with words, sometimes in song, sometimes simply reciting Scripture. I even incorporated it into my own little bedtime ritual with Doyle. Each night we would read a story, say a prayer, and then praise God together as we walked down the hallway toward his room.

But this night was different.

"One more story, Mommy?" he said, his big blue eyes staring up at me.

Dusk was falling outside and the chilly northern winds were beginning to usher in the first whispers of the coming winter as they picked up flurries of fallen leaves and scattered them, dancing across our front lawn.

"No, it's bedtime," I replied, gently but firmly.

"One more, Mommy?"

"It's getting dark, honey, it is time to say your prayers."

He was silent, considering his options as I lifted him off the couch and started walking with him down the hallway. He knew that throwing a fit wouldn't get him very far, but he was a toddler like any other, and I could tell that the temptation was rising within. Without thinking, I threw my arms up in the air, just as he did every night. "I love you, Jesus!" I declared with a smile.

In that instant, his whole face changed with the realization that his mother had stolen his line, banishing all thoughts of the injustice of bedtime. And without a moment's hesitation he took *my* part. After I turned out the light, I quickly went to look for George. He was in Allen and Phillip's room, restocking drug supplies.

"Did you just hear Doyle?" I asked.

He shook his head. "No. What happened?"

"He is learning to pray."

George stopped for a moment. "God is good to us."

And then it dawned on me. We'd only given our lives to the Lord a few years ago, and yet having a relationship with Jesus—something that had been so foreign to us for so long—was so normal to Doyle. The children were coming to know the Truth for themselves!

Later that night, I started thinking back along the journey, remembering the dear friends we had left behind in Florida and how far we had come since that first Sunday school meeting in the summer of 1965.

"George. I have been wondering about going back to Florida for a visit to see Sherry and the girls. What do you think?"

"I think you should go, Betty," he replied without hesitation. "I can manage the boys for a few days without you."

"I had in mind to take Phillip with me," I continued. "Don't you think some warm weather and the sea breeze might do his asthma some good?"

"It certainly couldn't hurt," he said after a moment's thought. "You should go—both of you!"

It was February 1968 when Phillip and I left Nashville under a blanket of rain, soaring through the frigid grey skies. The colors of the Florida landscape burst into life as soon as we landed, lit up so much more vividly than I remembered by the warm winter sunshine.

"It is so good to see you!" grinned Sherry as she met us

in the baggage area. "And who's your handsome traveling companion?" I was so anxious to see her, Marie, Velma, Nadine, and all the rest of the girls from the Bible study and to hear their news.

The following night we went together to a large Assembly of God church where Derek Prince happened to be speaking—just like old times! It was late, Phillip was tired, and Derek spoke for over an hour, covering a host of topics—from salvation to sanctification—and many things in between. As he reached his conclusion, he looked out over the crowded room, as was his custom, and invited the congregation to respond to his message by simply standing where they were and praying a prayer of commitment to the Lord.

Marie and I stood up, while Phillip repeatedly tugged on my shirt.

"Mommy, I want to do that!" he said in a loud whisper. "I want to pray that prayer."

He caught me by surprise. I had no idea he was awake, let alone coherent enough to even hear Derek's message and respond. Besides, Derek had touched on so many topics; I wasn't sure which one had captivated his five-year-old mind.

"What prayer do you want to pray, Phillip?" I asked. Phillip was standing on his chair.

"Mommy, didn't you hear what he said?" he asked. "I want to receive Jesus as my Savior!"

"Is that what you heard, Phillip?"

"Yes!" he replied simply.

I looked at Marie, who was grinning widely. There was no question that God was working in Phillip's life—the Holy Spirit was drawing him by the same irresistible grace that had first drawn us. And we were both overjoyed. God's ability to move in a life is not limited to age. He could reach Doyle at two and Phillip at five.

"Marie? Would you lead him?" I asked, choking up. I wanted to listen to Phillip's prayer.

Only when we were back in Murfreesboro did I wake up to the fact that Phillip hadn't experienced any asthmatic symptoms in days. At first I thought it was the Florida weather. But for six months, George and I had prayed faithfully for the enemy to take his hands off of Phillip. And now, all of a sudden, God had answered that prayer.

"God, when did this healing happen?" I asked myself in the kitchen one morning, thanking Him for once again surprising me with His goodness. And then I knew. It was as simple and profound as anything I had ever realized before: It was the night Phillip responded to the gospel in Florida.

The Cross of Christ is not only the place of salvation, I learned; it is the place of healing too.

• • •

SPRING CAME before we knew it, and so did the mid-week revival at St. Marks Methodist Church. Derek and Lydia stayed at the Imperial Motel on Broad Street, next door to Shoney's restaurant, knowing they would be more comfortable there than sharing the boys' twin beds at home.

Word about Derek's last visit had been shared in various church circles around the area, and we ourselves promoted it wherever we could. On a blustery Wednesday night in March, and in front of a sizable crowd, eleven people received Jesus as Savior. The second night Derek taught on healing. After the service, a well-known lady in the church came forward for prayer, tears welling up in her eyes. Her newborn grandchild was in the hospital in serious condition, and the doctors were uncertain if the baby would survive. The people remaining joined hands in prayer and prayed for the baby's health.

Just two and a half miles away in the county hospital that night, the little baby was miraculously healed. The last night, George and I decided to invite all those who had given their lives to the Lord that week to come to our house for dessert and coffee. We crowded into the living room, and while I served refreshments, Derek talked to the small group about a relationship with Jesus beyond just being religious. Something began in our home that changed our lives forever, though we had no idea of it at the time.

The next morning, George and I went to the motel to say goodbye to the Princes. When we arrived, their door was propped open and they were getting ready to leave. Derek was by the bed, helping Lydia with a suitcase.

George knocked on the open door, and Lydia looked up in surprise. "Betty and George!"

"We wanted to say good-bye and thank you," said George.

"It was our pleasure," said Derek, shaking George's hand.

"Betty, I wanted to thank you again for taking me shopping," Lydia said gratefully as she laid her new dresses neatly into the suitcase. Her eyes shone brightly.

"You're welcome," I replied. It was a pleasant break for me to take her to Goldstein's department store on the square. I knew it would mean a lot: America was still so new to Lydia after so many years living in Europe, the Middle East, and Africa. Besides, she was in her late 70s— not the easiest age to adapt to yet another culture.

"We have been praying that God would move in Tennessee in ways we experienced in Florida," I said as we got ready to leave. "Thank you for the time you have given to us and to this city."

Derek closed his suitcase and set it by the door. "Incidentally, Lydia and I went to breakfast with Rev. Moss this morning," he said.

"Really?" said George.

"That's nice," I replied.

"I told him you would be beginning a Bible study in your home."

"We would?" I was shocked and immediately glanced at George. Derek sure had a way of dropping a bomb. What did he mean? We had only been believers for two years. We were still learning ourselves. Surely he was mistaken. We weren't qualified, and *that* was the truth!

"Thank you," said George thoughtfully. I looked at him in disbelief. It was a big deal to start a Bible study. Not only were we beginners, but there was a certain exposure to holding meetings in your home. People just didn't do that in those days. No; church life functioned under the oversight of the denominations. By stepping outside those boundaries, you put yourself into the category of the weird, rebellious, and unknown. We were newcomers to this area, we were trying to start a business, and our friendships were still emerging. It was one thing in the cosmopolitan suburbs of Fort Lauderdale, Florida—but I wasn't so sure I wanted to deal with that in small-town Tennessee.

Yet at the same time—I knew we had been praying for God to move!

"Begin next week, on Thursday night. Then you won't be in competition with church programs," Derek continued in his matter-of-fact way. "Invite those who responded to the meeting, and see what happens."

Start next week already? We didn't have any material! Yet I admired the way Derek believed the Gospel and acted on it. It seemed so simple.

"Okay," I agreed, amazed at the words that came out of my mouth.

"We would like to pray for you," Lydia said. She joined hands with Derek and then took ours. We made a circle and bowed our heads to the Lord.

"God," Derek began, "I ask that you would guide George and Betty and give them great wisdom. And above all, use this Bible study to further your kingdom in this area. Amen."

"Have you ever considered the name Murfreesboro?" He looked straight up at us as he finished the prayer. "Names aren't passed down by chance you know. There's something even in the way you spell it. I think there will be freedom in this place!"

Before we knew it, Thursday rolled around. It had been quite a process to figure out what we should teach. We spent three or four nights by the side of our bed praying for guidance until finally, we decided to play a cassette tape about the Holy Spirit that Nadine had sent us from Florida.

Everything was ready: drinks and cookies on the table, chairs neatly arranged in a circle, the tape rewound in the player ready to start. Four couples showed up, all of them hungry to learn more after their experiences the week before. Among them was a couple who were both employed at the local college. Just a few days earlier, several people had been in our living room, and Derek had prayed a simple prayer for everyone. The wife's demeanor changed and a peace showed on her face. I was startled and shot a look of panic across the room at Lydia.

"Don't move," she cautioned gently. "God is working in that woman's life. Let it be."

And sure enough, something broke free, and she started laughing intermixed with joyful prayers: the great oppression that had dominated her life had broken with a simple prayer of surrender.

On the first night of the new Bible study, it was her husband's turn.

He was a quiet man and the purchasing agent for the college. He sat at the end of our yellow glasstop table in the kitchen and listened intently to the message, intrigued by his wife's description of her experience and impacted by the sudden change in her life the week before. He, like everyone else, huddled round, eyes focused on the slowly turning reels of the player as the spool of dark brown magnetic tape gradually shifted from one side to the other.

At the end of the lesson, the man looked up and said, "I want to surrender my life to God as never before."

As the months went by, the Bible study became the catalyst for so much of what God was doing in our lives. Each week George would do his best to rush home on

Thursday evenings. The boys were free to join in the meeting, which they often did. It was how they learned. Once in a while, an emergency call would come—a mare in foal or an accident at a stable. On those nights, I would have to cover the study on my own. But gradually, even I grew in confidence. We would search out taped messages throughout the week that we could listen to together and apply to our lives and that, after listening, would motivate us in prayer.

Above all, a love for people was birthed inside of us—a passion for helping them *know* Jesus. We had whites and blacks, Asians, Vietnamese, Jews, and Arabs attend the study over the years. Over time, it mattered less to us what people in the community thought—what mattered more were those who were finding a meaningful relationship with a living God.

We would pray for anyone.

One day later that summer, George was called out to a small stable just off Highway 96, on the way to Franklin. There was a two-year-old colt with a tendon problem that needed urgent attention. It was raining, and when he arrived the owner was visibly distressed. George kneeled down to examine the leg. He could smell the alcohol on the trainer. He was drinking heavier than usual. George treated the horse, mostly in silence. When George was finished with the horse, he gave the trainer some medication.

"If you ever want to deal with the stress in your life,

come see me at my home. I'll help you." George handed him a business card. "There's my address." And he left.

George told us about the man at the dinner table. As we said our blessing over our meal, we included him in the prayer.

Later that night, George and I stayed up talking. There were so many people that needed Jesus, I thought, remembering the lady at the saddle horse farm in Lebanon, "almost convinced" but "just not quite." We closed our eyes: "Father, help us not to waste our lives!" George prayed.

Early the next morning there was a knock on the door. On the doorstep was George's friend the trainer.

He said, "Doc, I need to talk to you. You said yesterday that if I wanted a change in my life to come see you. I'm ready to change," he said with tears in his eyes.

George said, "Come on in." The three of us sat down in the family room. We discussed his pressure and that the answer for him must start with a spiritual change. He agreed and was ready to change, so George led him in a simple prayer of salvation, sitting right there in the family room.

And so, person by person, God began answering our prayers for Middle Tennessee, one heart at a time. With every changed life, our connection to the community grew. Yet almost more than a year had passed, and we still hadn't found a place to build a clinic and a home. It wasn't that we were short of choices. It was just that none of the properties we looked at felt quite right.

By the fall, George's practice was steadily outgrowing our Scotland Acres home. I would lie awake at night running through the options. I didn't know how much longer the boys' room could serve as our pharmacy. Yet as much as I had desires and George had his opinions, I knew that the Lord had the perfect place in mind. We were learning to be still and let Him open the doors—if only we had the patience to wait.

So we looked, and we waited. And looked . . .

It was early October, 1968. The boys were asleep, and George and I were in our bedroom talking. It had been about seven months since we'd started the Bible study, and we had been praying for God to keep bringing us people with whom we could share Jesus. I glanced over at George. His eyes were closed and his hands were folded behind his head.

I was still kneeling by the side of the bed pondering the question of a piece of land, thinking back to the most recent property we had seen west of the city. It was on the Salem Highway, across the road from the Brown View Farm: an elegant white manor house with green shutters, white barns, and more than seven hundred acres of pristine pasture. The land we were looking at couldn't have offered a greater contrast. It was an overgrown, rather neglected, twenty-five-acre farm—sloping uphill from the road with a four-room white farmhouse and a large oak tree towering over the roof. Yet the more I thought about it, the more its potential shone through: a fresh stream ran in front of the property, with water clean enough to drink; limestone boulders and the occasional purple iris dotted the wooded landscape. There was an unpainted pole barn on the west side of the slope of the hill with plenty of space for a paddock, a clinic, and eventually a home.

"Thank you, Lord, that you will lead us with these properties," I prayed with a strong voice. "That we will make the right decision." George sat up, by now fully awake.

"Do you *have* to pray so loud?!" he snapped, while I just looked up at him in surprise. "What was *that* about?" I thought, not realizing that he'd fallen asleep.

All of a sudden we heard the sound of the doorbell. It was unusual for anyone to call so late at night. I pulled my dressing robe a little closer and went to answer the door.

"Why, Mr. Maples!" It was past nine o'clock in the evening, and our Realtor was standing outside.

"I'm so sorry to disturb you at this hour, Mrs. Jackson," he apologized, "But could I talk to Dr. Jackson for a minute? I have some news that I thought you would both want to hear before you went to bed."

"Of course. Come in. Come in. Just a minute. Let me go and get him."

I opened up the bedroom door. "George," I whispered. "It's Clark Maples. He needs to talk to us!" George quickly got dressed and followed me to the living room.

"Won't you sit down?" I asked the Realtor, motioning with my hand to one of the chairs.

"No, thank you. I'm fine. This will only take a few minutes. First, I would like to apologize for coming over so late, but I just received a phone call from Mrs. Taylor about her property on Salem Road. She's had an offer from a group of businessmen who want to develop the land. However, she told me just now that she would really like a family to have it—*your family*, in fact." He paused, shifting his gaze from George to me and back to George again. "If—of course—you would still like to buy it?

"I'm afraid, however, I need your decision no later than eight o'clock tomorrow morning," he concluded. "I know it isn't much time, but I thought you would at least want the night to think about it."

"We'll call first thing in the morning," George replied as he saw Mr. Maples out.

We went back to the bedroom and sat down. George and I were both quiet for a while as we thought through the options.

"It's everything we've been looking for, Betty. A good location, plenty of room, a stream, close to town, on a state highway." George ticked off each attribute on the fingers of his left hand. "The boys would love it!"

I thought about the small white farmhouse. Two bedrooms! It would be quite a squeeze for a family of five—and it would likely be a year or two before we could build. We both knew that the clinic simply had to be built first.

"Your dad could remodel the farmhouse, don't you think? Then start on the clinic," George suggested, as though he were reading my mind.

I nodded. My father had a construction company and was an excellent builder. Everything did seem to point to this property. All I could think of was how beautiful it could look and how ideal it would be for both George and the boys.

A moment passed in silence.

"I'm sorry I asked you not to pray so loud," George said quietly.

"It's okay," I said and started to giggle. I always laughed at the strangest moments.

"What's so funny?" George asked, about to become irritated again.

"God is!" I said as I climbed into bed next to George. "He has a sense of humor, don't you think?" I said, ducking my head underneath his outstretched arm. "I clearly wasn't praying too loudly for Him, was I?"

Early the next day, the deal was done. By mid-morning, George was already making arrangements with my father to begin renovating the house and then building the clinic. He was on the telephone excitedly drawing up plans: a building big enough for trucks to pull through

and unload sick horses, with showers and washroom fa-
cilities, surgical space, and stalls. Within a few more days,
we had put our house up for sale. There were fences to
build, land to be cleared, permits to acquire, lumber to
buy. Everything became a whir of activity and excitement.
In fact, we almost missed the letter.

It came just a few days later, accompanied by a bro-
chure in the mail—I looked it over, then kept it until the
boys were in bed.

"George," I said, after turning out the light in Allen
and Phillip's room. "Derek and Lydia are making a trip to
Israel at the end of November. They would like us to come
with them." I handed him the letter.

"To *Israel?*" George sounded surprised. "Betty, that's
six weeks from now." He stretched the letter out and began to read.

"They've asked us to pray about coming," George said.
"We need to at least do that."

"But what about the boys?" I asked, my heart beginning to beat faster. Ever since first hearing Derek's message in Florida on the eve of the Six-Day War, that tiny
nation had always been somewhere in the back of our
minds. When it came into the news, we paid more attention. When we looked at our Bible, we started noticing
that the name of Israel was everywhere. And it wasn't just
a spiritual concept—passage after passage spoke of Israel
as a place, filled with real people who one day would be

restored to their land and then, finally, to their God.

"Well, your parents will be here. Your dad has already agreed to work on the clinic and your mother is planning to come too."

"But three weeks is a long time to be away from the practice, isn't it, George?"

"I could lose some clients," he acknowledged. "That's why we need to pray. But if the Lord is inviting us to go, He'll take care of that, Betty."

I left the kitchen and followed George into the bedroom, where we both sat down on the bed. Amidst all my questions, there was an excitement inside. I agreed with him. It was an invitation from God we couldn't pass up!

"Heavenly Father," George prayed, "our lives have been bought with a price—they are yours. Our finances are yours; our practice is yours; our children are yours. Guide us, we pray. We want to know Your will. If this invitation is from You, don't let us miss it."

Scan this code with your camera-equipped
smartphone to view the companion video
for Chapter Ten. If you do not have the QR
app on your phone, visit your app store and
search for *QR code reader.*

ELEVEN

LIVING STONES

As you come to him, the living Stone—rejected by men but chosen by God and precious to him—you also, like living stones, are being built into a spiritual house to be a holy priesthood, offering spiritual sacrifices acceptable to God through Jesus Christ.
1 Peter 2:4–5 (NIV1984)

It was Friday, November 15, and at our house on Scotland Drive, there was much excitement. My parents had arrived a couple days earlier, our bags were packed, and last-minute instructions were written down.

Six-year-old Phillip sat with me after breakfast, and asked, "Mommy, when is it again that you leave for You-York?"

"After you have arrived at Miss Hopeful's kindergarten and Allen is in class at Reeves Rogers," I said. We again talked about the eighteen days we would be away, looking at the calendar together and thinking ahead to Thanksgiving with the grandparents in the house. Phillip seemed reassured as we recalled his days with my parents at the time of Doyle's birth. I reminded him that one day, soon after he returned from my parents' house we were eating cherry pie, and he said, "If I were at Grandpa's house, I would eat my pie sitting on his lap."

Two large suitcases standing near the door did not threaten three-year-old Doyle. He was delighted that his grandparents had arrived. He did not seem to know, nor did he care that we would be missing from the house for a few days. Allen felt comfortable too, as we had spent time over the past few days looking at maps together, and he understood the journey would be long.

Once we arrived at Kennedy International Airport, we met Christians from various states and many different denominations who were all thrilled at the opportunity to make the trip together. Our flight to London, which left in the early evening, was uneventful. Once the lights were out, I was pleased to curl up in George's lap feeling very relaxed after a few days of intense preparation. Arriving in London, we took a bus through the beautiful countryside of England to South Chard, where we were welcomed by a wonderful group of Christians.

Our hotel room was a short distance from the church Derek would be speaking at on Sunday. Our room had very little heat, but there was hot water in the shower and our bed had a delightful down-filled comforter . . . we slept like logs.

Monday, back in London, we visited the House of Parliament, the Tower of London, St. Paul's Cathedral, Scotland Yard, No. 10 Downing Street, Hyde Park, and

Westminster Abbey.

Preparing for the flight to Tel Aviv found us all in line again at the London airport, refreshed and rested, anticipating what was just ahead of us.

The plane's wheels touched the ground with a skid, and George and I found ourselves joining in the burst of applause that erupted across the cabin. We had landed safely in Tel Aviv. It was about six o'clock in the morning, and the sky was bright with the colors of the rising sun.

And now we were landing in Israel. I had spent the night with my New Testament open, anticipating all the new things we would see: where Jesus walked on water, where he fed the five thousand, where he died and rose again. Next to me, George had drifted off to sleep studying a map of the Holy Land which, even now, was unfolded on his lap. There was so much to learn.

The cabin doors opened, and we were greeted by a blast of warm Mediterranean air. It was early morning in November, yet the sun was already shining with surprising strength. Just ahead of me, as I descended the steps, an elderly Jewish gentleman bent to his knees, taking off his hat and pulling back the skirts of his long black coat. My heart surged as I watched him kiss the tarmac, tears streaming down his face. "Can this be true?" I thought to myself. "Are we really in Israel—the land of the Bible?"

The small arrivals hall was filled with noise and confusion. George and I stayed close together, trying to keep sight of Derek and Lydia through the crowd. It was a stark contrast to London, with its cool skies, grey people, and black umbrellas. Israel was a land bathed in *Technicolor.* It was as though someone had switched on the lights and turned up the volume. Everywhere voices were shouting and arms were waving. People were running to embrace each other, some with laughter, others with tears, none of them caring whether they were holding up a line of one hundred equally weary travelers behind.

It was just after seven by the time we left the terminal, led by a dark-haired man in his early thirties—our tour guide. He spoke with a thick, loud Middle Eastern accent and was holding a suede cowboy hat high above his head.

"Achshav. Come along!" he called impatiently, looking over our heads to the stragglers at the back of the group. All around us taxicabs and buses were jostling for position, riding on the curb and cutting each other off. It was a relief to get seated on the bus.

"Ladies and Gentlemen," he began, balancing in the aisle next to the driver while facing the back of the bus. "Welcome to Israel, the land of Promise: The Holy Land!" I couldn't help but smile as I looked out of the window and saw two taxi drivers standing on the curb below, shaking their fists wildly at each other, almost on the verge of blows. From where I was sitting, it didn't look very holy to me.

"My name is Yehuda. But in English you probably

know me better as Judah. Of course, for those of you who like rock and roll," he continued with a broad grin, "you can call me Jude!"

There was a ripple of laughter from the back of the bus as he started humming "Hey Jude"—the smash hit Beatles single that had topped the music charts the previous summer—into the microphone. The musical allusion went over my head, but I laughed all the same. His carefree manner managed to put us all instantly at ease.

"You're tired, so I won't sing anymore just now. There will be time for that," he carried on, clearly reveling in the fact that he had a captive audience. "We're now on our way to the Galilee and have a full day of sightseeing ahead. But first some ground rules: Stay together. Don't go wandering off on your own. There are still many landmines left unexploded from the war, and we want you to stay safe at all times. Don't eat the food sold by the side of the road, and do not drink from public water fountains, no matter how thirsty you get. It's not worth getting sick!"

The rich, dreamy sea breeze mingled with so many colorful sights and vibrant sounds: tall date palms and bright pink bougainvilleas; young boys by the side of the road selling long, curved loaves of sesame bread or bags of freshly baked pita. And yet, as the bus pulled away, all I could see beyond the airport perimeter was a stark, burnt, treeless landscape.

Israel in 1968 was a primitive, war-torn place. There

were few modern roads; most were pot-holed, one-lane highways, and our driver, an Arab Christian from Nazareth, would often have to pull over onto the gravel shoulder to allow the oncoming traffic to pass. Through the open windows, we kept hearing unfamiliar sounds as we passed from town to town; the harsh yet musical consonants of Hebrew in one place would blend with the shrill rapidity of Arabic in the next. And there was security everywhere: young soldiers with machine guns slung across their backs—men and women—some of them barely eighteen years of age.

We stopped briefly to see the ruins of the ancient Roman port city of Caesarea (very little of which had been excavated in those days), the bustling modern-day port of Haifa, before climbing in the Carmel mountain range where Elijah confronted the prophets of Baal. To the west, we could see the vast expanse of the Mediterranean stretching toward the horizon. To the southeast, the Jezreel Valley, sloping down toward a great rift in the earth, where it slipped out of sight into the Jordan River ravine. As we stood as a group looking over the Jezreel Valley, knowing that it was at this location where the battle of Armageddon would be fought, I could not hold back the tears. I knew what this would mean to so many who would not be prepared to meet God.

As we left the coast and approached Tiberius, the scenery changed. The soil became more fertile as we descended to below sea level, through rugged limestone hills, toward the calm freshwater basin. There were rows of eucalyptus trees not far from the water's edge, but little else. Beyond them, through the afternoon haze on the other side of the sparkling lake, we could make out the faint outline of the Golan Plateau.

"It's breathtaking," I said.

George just nodded at first, lost in the view. "How did *you* imagine it Betty?" he asked a few moments later.

"I don't know."

I'd heard stories about this lake from childhood. Jesus had calmed the storm, fished with His disciples, fed five thousand, and here we were. Yet the images imprinted on my mind were still those from the picture books I'd read as a child. Now I could see for myself the light dancing in the shallows; the rocky, sun burnt hills; the winding roads and small fishing villages. It was a real place. The lake was smaller than I had expected . . . how could it have survived the years and made such an impact on so many lives and still be something that we could see with our eyes?

We continued along the edge of the water until we reached a fork in the road. To the right, the highway dropped off and continued to head eastward toward Capernaum on the northern shore. The bus, meanwhile, continued straight ahead, beginning a steep, winding ascent away from the lake and up to a grey-domed church perched on the summit of a rounded hillside overlooking the northwest corner of the Sea of Galilee.

As we disembarked, I was struck by the tranquility of the scene. Franciscan nuns were tending to the terraced gardens that surrounded the black basalt entrance to the church. It was a quiet, yet lonely, place. Tall Italian cypress trees were flanked by bright orange canna lilies, alive with color in the afternoon sun. Walking through the monastery grounds, it looked like something out of a picture book of Tuscany or Rome.

Yehuda, our guide, gathered us together in the shade of the portico. The current church was just thirty years old, he informed us—commissioned by Italian dictator Benito Mussolini just before the outbreak of the Second World War.

"Yet Christians have worshipped at this site for some sixteen hundred years," he continued. "The hill is simply known as the Mount of Beatitudes, because it is here that Jesus gave the famous teaching recorded in the fifth chapter of Matthew's gospel, 'Blessed are the poor and meek. . . .'"

Yehuda began leading us away from the church and toward a dark stone wall that bordered the gardens. Beyond the wall was a field that sloped down the hillside toward the shore. It opened out onto one of the most beautiful views of the lake I could imagine.

"We remember this place because of Jesus' Sermon on the Mount," he began. "Imagine Jesus speaking here for hour after hour to thousands without a microphone or a bullhorn. How could that have been possible?"

I looked at George, intrigued.

"The truth is that you can stand here at the top and hear two people talking way off in the distance at the foot of the hill. At the same time you can also stand by the shore and hear us talking now. The Galilee isn't just a lake. It is a canvas on which an Almighty God painted this scenery. Before the beginning of time, He shaped these hills and molded these rocks into the natural amphitheater you see before you now."

It was late afternoon by the time we drove into Tiberius. The sun was already beginning to dip below the ridge of western hills, illuminating the barren contours of the Golan Heights through the haze with spectacular shades of red, pink, and orange. As we wound our way through the narrow streets, I looked into the windows of the apartment buildings that were sparsely stacked like terraces into the side of the hill, and I could see the dim lights of television sets flickering in every one. As we approached the center of the town, I could see half a dozen small shops dotted by the shore, a tiny dock, and a few small fishing boats. It was a primitive, unpopulated place.

The bus pulled up outside a three-story concrete building, set back about three blocks from the water. It looked a little more like a school to me than a hotel, but at that point I was so tired I could have slept on the shore. We disembarked from the bus and walked into the lobby, where a large crowd of Israelis were standing around a small black and white television set, intently watching the evening news.

"They sure watch a lot of TV around here!" George remarked. But I just shrugged my shoulders. It was in Hebrew and we couldn't understand a word of it, so we headed to our room.

"How can we take it all in!" I exclaimed.

"I guess we'll have to come back again," George replied casually, unaware at the time of the significance of his words.

I awoke early the next morning, sometime between four and five o'clock. Stepping out of bed quietly, trying not to disturb George, I walked across the room and pulled a bathrobe out of the suitcase. The temperature had dropped in the night, and I could feel the fresh morning breeze drifting off the lake and in through the open window. I pulled up a chair and sat there, looking out, as the deep blues of the eastern sky gradually turned to grey.

Soon there was enough light to read, so I picked up my New Testament, scanning the pages to find Jesus' words from the Sermon on the Mount that were still echoing in my ears from the previous afternoon. But my eyes stopped a few paragraphs short:

> *Leaving Nazareth, he went and lived in*
> *Capernaum, which was by the lake in the area of*

Zebulun and Naphtali—to fulfill what was said through the prophet Isaiah:

"Land of Zebulun and land of Naphtali, the way to the sea, along the Jordan, Galilee of the Gentiles—the people living in darkness have seen a great light; on those living in the land of the shadow of death a light has dawned."
(Matthew 4:13–16 NIV)

I thought back to the emptiness I felt walking out of St. Mary's Hospital in Rochester—knowing that my body was healed but that I had nothing of eternal value to leave as a legacy for my children. It was a bleak, hopeless place, the "land of the shadow of death"—I'd been there. And it was for people like me, living in the midst of such darkness and futility, that Jesus came. Not to the big cities of the Roman world—to the nobles and governors of Athens, Ephesus, or Rome—but to a tiny backwater fishing village on the edge of the Empire. I could hear His words up there on the hillside, just a few short miles away, proclaiming a blessing over the poor, the meek, and the hungry.

Shortly after eight o'clock the whole group was gathered on the bus. I wasn't the only one who had awakened before dawn, and all around me our newfound friends were chatting excitedly as we traveled the short distance to the shoreline and held a brief time of worship by the edge of the dock. Before long, a boat appeared that carried us across the water to Capernaum.

The weather was perfect: warm air, clear skies. The water was calm, and the haze that had hovered over the surrounding hills the previous day had evaporated. It was so beautiful. We stood together there on the deck in wonderment of these words: *On those living in the land of the shadow of death a light has dawned.*

The boat docked close to Capernaum. There we saw the broken foundation walls of a fisherman's house amongst the rubble of some old ruins of ancient homes that stood between the ancient Synagogue and the sea. It didn't look like much, just a few rocks by the side of a lake. But in the years following Jesus' death, this became the focal point of Christian worship in the area. Years of archeological study had led to one inescapable conclusion: this must have been the very neighborhood, the home of Simon Peter, where the roof on the house was removed by his friends so a man who could not walk was lowered to Jesus.

Back on the bus again, we retraced our steps up past the Mount of Beatitudes, leaving the lake far behind as the highway twisted and turned up the steep rocky incline into the Upper Galilee, close to the old "green line" that—from 1948 until the recent war of June '67—had marked the makeshift border between Israel and Syria. We were entering the Hula Valley: an open expanse of fertile fields bordered on one side by the Naphtali Mountains and on the other by the western ridge of the Golan Heights. It had been less than eighteen months since Israeli forces had overwhelmed the Syrian tank brigades mustered on that ridge and secured the high ground east of the Galilee all the way up north to the peak of Mount Hermon. And all around us the signs of the conflict were plain to see: abandoned artillery cannons strewn along the side of the highway, sandbagged bunkers nestled in razor wire. Gone were the ancient stones that littered the holy sites of Capernaum, the faded Byzantine mosaics of Tabgha, the tranquil views of the lake from the beach where the resurrected Jesus prepared breakfast for His disciples. Instead we saw the burned-out hulls of jeeps and tanks left over from the Six-Day War.

The mood of the group grew reflective, even somber.

I studied our guide, sitting just a few rows ahead of us, feet stretched out into the aisle and a faraway look on his face as he followed the landscape with his eyes. He couldn't have been a year or two older than George, and yet his life had been filled with war.

"To your left," he said, turning in his seat and projecting his voice all the way to the back, "we're passing the medieval hilltop town of Safed. Since the sixteenth century, it has been a vibrant center of Jewish thought and learning. You know the rhyme?" He stood up with a mischievous grin. "In fourteen-hundred and ninety-two . . ."

"Columbus sailed the ocean blue!" we all echoed in reply.

"You guys are smart," he quipped. "But what you may not know is that in the year 1492, King Ferdinand and Queen Isabella also exiled the Jews of Spain. At the time it was one of the largest Jewish communities in Europe. Some stayed and endured terrible persecution. But others fled to the only place they knew that their people had ever known freedom. They came to Israel, and many of them settled right here . . ." His voice trailed off. There was silence for a moment, and then he started speaking to the driver in Hebrew, pointing up to the hills and waving his hands with an urgency in his voice. The bus pulled over onto the gravel by the side of the road, close to the small Israeli village of Hatzor.

"This is where I fought," he said, after leading us off the bus to see a small stone memorial that had been erected by the side of the road. "We were moving up that hill, in the thick of the battle. It was night and we were completely outnumbered. We blew out the bridge in front of us so the enemy tanks couldn't advance. And we fought hand-to-hand up the hill. We could hear the shots, but nothing hit us. It was amazing.

"And that's when we saw the figures in white . . ."

"Who?"

"The men in white."

"But who were they?"

Yehuda shrugged, his eyes still fixed on the ridge across the valley.

"Do you have any explanation?" Derek inquired.

"All I know is that we won," the young Israeli said, motioning us back on the bus. "Come on, people," he joked, his tone suddenly changing, "we don't have all day!"

We stared out of the windows at the hills. Thousands of years had passed, but the God of Heaven was still watching over His people. This place was a miracle. That was the truth!

It was not until the following day that we began the three-hour journey south, stopping first in Nazareth before passing the bleak, barren slopes of Mount Gilboa, where King Saul took his last fateful stand against the armies of the Philistines. After this the road narrowed and continued to descend through the arid landscape of the Jordan Valley until we reached the ancient oasis of Jericho on the northern edge of the Dead Sea. Even in November, the desert heat was overpowering. This was the lowest place on earth, we learned: the oldest inhabited city in the world, and the historic gateway to the Promised Land. Only two years earlier, the town was under Jordanian occupation, standing guard, as it had done for thousands of years, over the waters of the lower Jordan River and the steep eastern ascent to Jerusalem.

"Now when Joshua was near Jericho," Derek began, as we stood on the ancient Tel a mile or so away from the bustling market town, *"he looked up and saw a man standing in front of him with a drawn sword in his hand. Joshua went up to him and asked, "Are you for us or for our enemies?"*

> *"Neither," he replied, "but as commander of the army of the LORD I have now come." Then Joshua fell facedown to the ground in reverence, and asked him, "What message does my Lord have for his servant?" The commander of the LORD's army replied, "Take off your sandals, for the place where you are standing is holy." And Joshua did so.* (Joshua 5:14–15 NIV)

Standing there, looking at the excavations of the ancient ruins, there was something strange and unfamiliar about the passage. I knew the story of Joshua and Jericho—everyone did: how the people marched round the walls in silence for six days, and on the seventh let out a mighty shout. We saw the evidence, pieced together stone-by-stone by archeologists over the decades: how the walls had fallen and been burnt in a single day; how the city had lain in ruins for centuries after the conquest. Everything seemed to fit the biblical record. And yet I had never realized that the "Commander of the Lord's army" did not come to fight on Joshua's side. In fact, he approached the Israelite camp with a drawn sword in his hand.

"There has only ever been one requirement for entrance to the Holy Land," Derek continued simply, "to take off your shoes!"

I looked around at the harsh, dusty landscape with its sharp rocks and steep paths and winced at the thought of walking barefoot here.

"You see, a Holy Land is for a Holy People," Derek stated plainly. "A Holy God *demands* righteousness. He demanded it from the Children of Israel as they emerged from forty years of wandering in the wilderness. And He demands it of each one of us today.

"Yet, as the prophet Isaiah realized, 'all our righteous acts are like filthy rags.' We can only stand in *His* righteousness by taking off our shoes—by laying down our own efforts, our own achievements and our own desires. We lay them down at the Cross. We enter the land of God's Promise by humbling ourselves before Him.

"The same is true of the people of Israel today. By God's miraculous grace and in His sovereign timing, the Jewish people have returned to their ancient homeland; their 'land of Promise.' We've even heard how the hosts of Heaven fought on their behalf!" He glanced over at Yehuda, who was staring off into the distance beyond the date palms of Jericho to the mountains of Moab, pretending not to listen.

"But the Commander of the Army of the Lord still comes to the Israelite camp with a drawn sword in His hand. He hasn't come to join in. He's come to take charge! He's calling them to take off their shoes. Why? Because He Himself took off His own, laid aside His power and majesty, and came to earth to die for their sins. My friends—the future of this land is inextricably linked with the identity of the Man with the drawn sword in His hand: Christ Jesus."

It had been twenty years since Derek and Lydia had left Israel. Derek spoke with a compassion and an understanding of the importance of present-day Israel that linked us with its past. George and I were conscious of a new and better understanding of Israel from that moment onward.

The sun was already beginning to cast deep shadows across the eastern slopes of the Judean hills as we began the breathtaking ascent to Jerusalem on the ancient Jericho road, a road that twisted and turned through steep rocky crevices and ravines, climbing almost four thousand feet from the shore of the Dead Sea in less than twenty miles. Jesus would have walked this way dozens of times in His lifetime, through the unrelenting desert heat. It was the perfect setting for the parable of the Good Samaritan. Behind every boulder I could imagine the faces of thieves who lived in the caves that dotted the sheer cliffs on either side of the road. And I too could relate to the fear of being ambushed and left for dead.

Once in a while, the bus would crest an incline and the slow, laboring ascent would pick up speed as a vista of golden dune-like hills would open up before us, each one taller than the next. On either side we passed tented Bedouin encampments that appeared not to have changed in more than four thousand years. The men sat and visited in the entrances to their elaborate camel-skin tents while their young children climbed the hills, chasing herds of wiry goats that were rummaging through the sparse vegetation for food.

And then I saw it, looming in the distance, the peak of a hill that was taller than the rest, silhouetted against the late afternoon sun with a tall spire extending straight upward toward the sky. My heart skipped a beat, as Yehuda told us we were catching our first sight of the Mount of Olives. I felt a strange sensation that I didn't understand. At the front of the bus, Yehuda began to hum softly to himself. The chatter of conversation quickly died down as everyone strained to hear the haunting folk tune and strangely melodic words, which seemed to increase in passion and volume the longer he sang.

> *Yerushalayim shel zahav*
> *Ve-shel nehoshet ve-shel or*
> *Ha-lo le-khol shirayikh*
> *Ani kinnor.*

"Tell us about that song," Lydia asked in the silence that followed.

"It was a big hit in the summer of '67," Yehuda replied thoughtfully, his typical bravado somewhat subdued. "It's called "Jerusalem of Gold," and it was released—by chance—just weeks before the war broke out. It's a song that speaks of our people's ancient longing for Jerusalem: how the city lies deserted, her cisterns empty and her walls abandoned. It's a lament. But all that changed when our paratroopers liberated the Old City and blew the shofar at the Western Wall. The author even added another verse in celebration!"

Suddenly without warning the bus became a choir led by an Episcopal Priest with a melodious voice:

> *Come, we that love the Lord,*
>   *And let our joys be known;*
> *Join in a song with sweet accord,*
>   *Join in a song with sweet accord*
> *And thus surround the throne,*
>   *And thus surround the throne.*
> Refrain
> *We're marching to Zion,*
> *Beautiful, beautiful Zion;*
> *We're marching upward to Zion,*
> *The beautiful city of God.*
> *Then let our songs abound,*
>   *And every tear be dry;*
> *We're marching through Immanuel's ground,*

We're marching through Immanuel's ground,
To fairer worlds on high,
  To fairer worlds on high.
We're marching to Zion,
Beautiful, beautiful Zion;
We're marching upward to Zion,
The beautiful city of God.

The bus continued to climb, weaving now through empty narrow streets until the walled city of Jerusalem suddenly came into view. It was some distance below us, across a steep valley gorge on an elevated plateau, encircled with hills and ablaze with light as the sun flashed off its domes, crosses, and spires. Flat-roofed, limestone-clad buildings sprawled out as far as the eye could see, flushed pink by the deep golden rays of the setting sun.

It was Friday evening, so the Jewish Sabbath was about to begin. There were few cars on the streets; no one was walking. The city looked so quiet and peaceful; it was breathtaking! But something was going on at the front of the bus. Our guide was leaning forward and speaking rapidly with our driver in animated tones. As he did, both men bent their ears close to the radio, adjusting the signal to pick up the news.

Suddenly we heard the roar of an army jeep pulling up beside us. Two soldiers sat in the front, flagging us down, while a third sat in the back holding a machine gun menacingly in the air. The bus pulled over, and Yehuda leapt out and started talking with the officer in much the same way that he had been speaking with our driver—arms waving, fingers pointing—both men talking simultaneously and yet apparently content that each was being heard. I looked questioningly at George—what was going on?

He climbed back onto the bus. "We're going straight to the hotel," he said briskly, with a somber look on his face. It was clear by now that we were no longer heading toward the summit of the Mount of Olives as planned, and the "Palm Sunday" walk down to the Garden of Gethsemane was going to have to be postponed. "There's been a bombing in the city. Everything is in lockdown until they find out who did it. No exceptions. That means you walk straight into the hotel, you eat your dinner, you go to bed. You do not leave the hotel. In the morning, we come out of the hotel, walk back onto the bus, and leave. You understand?"

Then it dawned on George. "That must have been why they were all gathered around the TV in Tiberius," he whispered.

● ● ●

"WHAT WAS THAT?"

It was the middle of the night, and I woke with a start.

There was silence. Then it came again: a loud ka-boom—like the sound of cannon fire.

"George!" I screamed, my heart pounding as I clung to him as tightly as I could. All sorts of thoughts raced across my mind. "George! Wake up!"

"I'm awake," he calmly replied. There was an overpowering tension in the air.

"We're being attacked!" I whispered in terror as I tried to move even closer to George under the covers, pushing him yet farther toward the edge of the bed.

"Just wait and see," George replied calmly, "but I don't think anyone is attacking us."

We both listened for a few more seconds in silence before the music came: an eerie, screeching sound that echoed loudly through the night. I put a pillow over my head to block out the noise. It was several minutes until it finally ended, but by then I was too shaken to go back to sleep. Before long, day began dawning outside. We quickly got dressed and went down to breakfast. I found Lydia and sat down.

"What was all that commotion last night?" I asked her as she sat drinking an early morning cup of tea.

"It was the Muslim call to prayer," she replied. "We used to be awakened by it every day before dawn when I lived with children in Ramallah. It's just part of life here." Lydia smiled. "It's Ramadan, Betty: the one month they set aside each year for fasting and prayer. The cannon fire you heard is part of the festival. They can eat before sunrise, so they wake sometime before five, say their prayers, have a meal, and get started with their day."

"Is the city still on lockdown?"

"It is, Betty, but it isn't that unusual. Life carries on. Ramadan always brings with it a period of tension—hundreds of millions of Muslims around the world going without food or water for twelve to fifteen hours at a time. They feast after sundown—and again at predawn. Everything will be back to normal tonight."

She was right. After breakfast we all filed onto the bus and headed out of the deserted city, passing nothing more than a lone donkey wandering in the street. The bus didn't stop until we had traversed the southwestern rim of the Judean hills and reached the Elah Valley—the area where David fought Goliath. In the midst of a field, we found a brook, a creek, perhaps like one where the young shepherd boy stooped down to collect five smooth stones with which to face the giant. More than all the churches and ruins, those small pebbles seemed to speak with greater volume than anything else we had seen or heard. I thought of the boys and picked some up.

I missed them so much, and I knew George missed them too.

Later that evening George and I were sitting in the hotel lobby with Derek and Lydia. It had been a long day that had taken us south to Beersheba and back up through the Judean wilderness via the ancient Dead Sea caves of Qumran. When we returned later that day, the lockdown was over, just as Lydia had said it would be. The crime had been solved. Most of the tour group had decided to call it a night soon after dinner, but we were still trying to absorb everything we had seen, and we lingered there in the lobby for a few minutes more.

"How did you enjoy your day?" Lydia asked.

"I took five small stones from the Elah brook," I ventured. "I thought George and I could take them back for the boys."

"You know, you can buy slingshots in the Old City too," Derek offered with a smile. "There's a verse in Psalm 102 which speaks about God arising and having mercy on Zion," Derek continued, quite serious now. "That there will come a time to favor her—a time of restoration and rebuilding. And in that day, the Word of God says, His servants will take pleasure in her stones and show favor to her dust. The dust and stones of this land are precious, but even more precious are the people! They are the living stones."

The Old City of Jerusalem was nothing like I imagined: a jumbled mixture of Roman ruins, Crusader churches, and bustling markets all thrown together in a maze of covered streets and passageways. The Arab street vendors sold olive wood Bibles or jewelry, refusing to take no for an answer as they joked, flattered, and cajoled their customers into a sale. It was noisy, vibrant, and bewildering. One of them even asked George if he would trade me for seven camels!

"Now if he had offered me seven horses, it would have been a done deal, Betty," George said a little later, a glint in his eye.

Everything changed as we walked through the ancient Jewish Quarter. Everywhere, we saw ransacked houses and burnt synagogues. During the 1948 War of Independence—our guide told us—the Arab Legions went through the area erasing more than a thousand years of Jewish life and worship. For nineteen hundred years, they had no access to their homes, their synagogues or the Western Wall of the ancient Temple Mount—the holiest place of Jewish prayer. Now, less than two years after ending the Jordanian occupation, Israeli stone masons and Arab carpenters were working side-by-side, rebuilding and renovating once more.

> *Then the nations around you that remain will know that I the LORD have rebuilt what was destroyed and have replanted what was desolate. I the LORD have spoken, and I will do it.*
> (Ezekiel 36:36 NIV)

We began a steep descent, on foot, catching a breathtaking view of the bronze-topped Dome of the

Rock and the slopes of the Mount of Olives beyond. Soon the Western Wall plaza opened up before us. We watched thin Orthodox Jewish men dressed in Russian fur hats and long-sleeved coats walking rapidly to prayer in the warm evening sun. They all looked the same, with their thick, dark-rimmed glasses, tasseled sideburns, and beards, seemingly oblivious to us and the rest of the world around them. On the other side of the partition, I could see their wives and daughters wearing dark brown wigs, rocking strollers and baby carriages with their toddlers and young children straggling behind.

As we walked toward the massive stones, stacked more than sixty feet in the air, we began to hear the whispered hum of a hundred murmured prayers. The men bent at the waist, nodding forward repetitively, kissing their prayer books with fervent devotion. On the women's side, they pressed tightly against the wall, shoving folded paper prayers into large rock crevices between the stones.

Derek briefly called the group together. "When Solomon built the first Temple in this place, he prayed a remarkable prayer: that whenever a foreigner comes here from a distant land and prays towards the temple, his requests would be granted. In this way the whole world would know the God of Israel is the one true God.

"These stones have no power of themselves," Derek continued, "but they stand as a reminder that the God of history has tied His name and reputation to this city and this people. We are foreigners—'aliens and strangers,' the Apostle Paul calls us in Ephesians 2. Yet we who were 'far off' have been brought near through the shed blood of His Son, their Messiah, Jesus Christ. 'And in him you too are being built together to become a dwelling in which God lives by his Spirit.'

"So Solomon's prayer still stands. We can come boldly to the Lord in prayer—even here today—not based on our own works of righteousness, but because of His abundant grace and mercy. And we can pray with confidence, knowing that He hears us and will grant us anything that we ask for in His Name."

It was getting late, the sun was about to set as George and I parted ways, he to the men's section on the left and I to the other side of the partition on the right. I pulled out my pocket New Testament and turned to Ephesians 2 as I went forward to touch the ancient stones.

> *For He Himself is our peace, who has made both one, and has broken down the middle wall of separation,* (Ephesians 2:14)

The physical partition I saw between male and female, the separation I felt from the Jewish women all around me—it had all been broken down in the person of Jesus. I no longer felt superior to them in the midst of all their empty traditions; I felt a deep compassion and love. I waited until George returned, and we stood quietly, then George prayed, "Lord, don't let us waste our lives. We want to follow you. Help us to love the Jewish people as you do!"

Scan this code with your camera-equipped smartphone to view the companion video for Chapter Eleven. If you do not have the QR app on your phone, visit your app store and search for **QR code reader.**

TWELVE

A WISE INVESTMENT

*Start children off on the way they should go,
and even when they are old they will not turn
from it.* **Proverbs 22:6 (NIV)**

Allen and Phillip were lifting their bicycles into the station wagon, and Doyle stood patiently by his *Radio Flyer* wagon, waiting for somebody to help him lift it in. This was the last load before we moved over to the farm on the Salem Highway. The clinic was finished, the white house remodeled. All that was left for us to do was move in.

I took a last look over the house in Scotland Acres and climbed into the passenger seat, balancing a chocolate cake on my lap, while George helped the boys squeeze in between the last remaining boxes and bags in the back.

The boys were silent at first, but their mood lightened quickly. They had been looking forward to this day ever since we were away in Israel the previous fall, when my father had first come down from Missouri to start working on the clinic. Week by week they had gone out to the property and watched with excitement as he laid the concrete blocks and then added the roof joists and siding. There was a small office, a shower, sinks, surgical stock, and a large open examination area.

We turned into the newly paved driveway. The dirt tracks and mud that had surrounded the clinic during the months of construction were all gone, and in their place a thick bed of straw was covering a layer of freshly sown grass seed. The white board fence was constructed and freshly painted. Comanche Sue—the bay mare that George had bought just a few days after Phillip was born—was already at home there, grazing contentedly in the pasture beyond. George was beaming: our dream was coming true.

Inside, the little white house had been completely remodeled. It was far smaller than we were accustomed to, with a kitchen so tiny that we couldn't even fit a table inside. So my father had come up with the idea of building a counter, lengthwise, along one of the walls. It was quite a sight, the five of us eating dinner in a long line, facing the wall. The master bedroom was more like a pantry; the doors permanently cracked open due to the size of the bed. And the three boys were sharing the second bedroom: three single beds, three little desks, and three chairs. Looking back, I suppose it might have been a sacrifice, but at the time, we didn't think of it that way. We were in a place George had longed for. A place he had wanted to rear our three boys.

The boys spilled out onto the back patio while I searched for a knife in an open box on the kitchen counter. Doyle was proudly wearing his new cowboy hat when I emerged with his cake and five paper plates.

"Happy Birthday, Doyle!" we all echoed in chorus, as George struggled to keep the candles lit in the breeze.

A few moments later the boys had finished their generous slices of birthday cake and Doyle was opening his last remaining gift from us: two western-style sheriff shirts to match the boots and the hat.

"Look, Phillip," he declared proudly, "I'm the sheriff!" Phillip was more interested in trying out his bike on the driveway and quickly followed after Allen, who was already racing down the incline at breakneck speed.

It didn't bother Doyle. He headed to the big white pole barn with his red wagon.

"I wonder what he's up to?" I thought, collecting the leftover cake and taking it back into the house. A few minutes later, I saw him emerge again, as I looked out of the kitchen window, a triumphant look all over his face.

"Mother, look!" He was pulling something in the wagon, waving furiously and yelling at the top of his voice. A few seconds later he abandoned his cargo on the lawn and came tearing into the house, breathless. Peeping out over the wagon's sides, I could see the noses of four or five puppies, standing on their hind legs, looking out.

"Mother. Red had puppies!"

Red was a shorthaired red mutt; a stray dog who lived in the barn. She had been dumped on the property in the months before we moved in, and the boys had been quick to adopt her.

"Come look," Doyle said leading me out the back door, anxious not to leave them alone for one second. "This is Blackie 1. This is Blackie 2. The little one here is Brownie. Then there is White—he's the one with the white spots. And then there's Baby Red. He looks just like his mother." I looked at my family: Doyle brimming over with excitement at the sight of five new puppies, Allen and Phillip tearing up and down the driveway on their bikes, and George out in the pasture checking on Comanche Sue. "It is unbelievable how much our life has changed!" I thought.

As the weeks passed, life settled back into a familiar routine, but everything had changed. For the first time in their lives, the boys were experiencing the freedom of life in the country outside the confines of paved sidewalks and back fences. It had opened up a whole new world of nature and adventure for them.

I remember one day kneeling by the back porch weeding some zinnias, hearing shouts of excitement as George drove the tractor through the pasture with the boys perched on the draw bar. Already in June, the humidity was high and the mosquitoes were out. I stood up to wipe the sweat from my forehead and saw the tractor slowing down, Phillip and Doyle behind George on the back draw bar, holding on tight and cheering Allen on as he dismounted to open the gate.

"Doyle is truly fearless," I thought, as I watched his excited face light up from a distance, recalling a conversation I had witnessed between him and our new housekeeper Jesse just a few days earlier. Jesse was a woman who had started working for us shortly before the move, cleaning and ironing and helping watch Doyle when I was busy at the clinic during the day. She was tall and kind, and we had all quickly grown to love her like one of the family. But she had a lot of fear in her life.

"No, Doyle," she'd told him firmly. "You know Jesse doesn't want you playing outside today." Ever since we had known Jesse, she was afraid to be alone in the house, even in the daytime.

Doyle didn't say a word in reply. He simply got a stool, walked over to the tall bookcase, and pulled down his picture Bible. At four years old, he understood that Jesse was afraid, but in his child-like way he couldn't understand why.

"Jesse," he said, flipping through the pages and pointing to a picture of Satan tempting Jesus in the wilderness, "Who's this?"

"Why, that's the devil!" Jesse answered.

Doyle looked down and began turning the pages again until he found a picture of Jesus. "And who is this?" he asked, his hands on each hip waiting for a reply.

"Jesus."

"Who's stronger, Jesse?"

"Well, Jesus . . . ?" said Jesse, hesitantly, not entirely sure what her four-year-old teacher was getting at.

"Jesse, you do not have to be afraid anymore. I'm going out to play!" And off he went, marching out the back door to play outside on his own. Jesse watched him through the window for a few moments, a thoughtful expression on her face. Then she broke out into a broad grin, nodded her head, heaved a big sigh, and went out to join him.

"Who's stronger, Jesse?" she muttered under her breath as he left the house, shaking her head in disbelief. "Then I'm going out to play!"

Jesse never had that fear again.

I looked back toward the paddock. Allen was already on the ground waiting for the tractor to pass before he could close the first gate. The race was on. With the throttle down, George charged through the gap and started to make a wide turn while Allen followed the line of the fence, beating the tractor comfortably and swinging the second gate open before his father even had to begin thinking of slowing down.

"Faster, Daddy!" Phillip was yelling as his older brother finished bolting the second gate and started gaining on them from behind. George continued speeding toward the barn while the younger boys kept shouting and laughing, heads turned to watch Allen, who by now was running at a full sprint only ten yards behind. Could he catch them? From where I was standing I couldn't quite see, but it was clear from the noise that George was enjoying the contest just as much as the boys.

Then there was a shout. Not a yell of laughter or a squeal of delight, but an urgent, chilling cry; the kind that any parent can recognize in an instant. The voice was Allen's, but my eyes were on Phillip, who in that brief second of laughter had lost his footing on the draw bar. Everything froze. Time went into slow motion as his hands flailed frantically, grabbing the air, clutching for anything to hold onto. But it was too late. Dangerously off balance, he rocked to one side and his right leg slipped in between the chassis and the wheel. I watched powerless as the motion of the tractor propelled him above the tire, his screams muffled as his body was thrown forward like a rag doll.

"George!" I gasped but I was too far away for him to hear me, and too terrified to give full throat to my cry. Allen was still sprinting toward the others, even faster now. Phillip's leg was trapped between the tractor tire and fender. His little body was propelled forward toward the ground. As he was lifted into the air, his arm hit George on the shoulder. Miraculously George stopped the tractor before crushing Phillip. And for the first time we could hear Phillip crying, "Daddy, it is hurting."

To this day there is no question in my mind that God saved Phillip's life in those seconds his body was caught up in that tire. In no time at all, George had leaped from the seat and was on his knees examining the leg, which by now was firmly wedged between the wheel and the tractor fender.

"God, we need you here right now," Doyle, looking up toward Heaven, demanded through his tears.

"Oh Lord, help George!" I cried beneath my breath.

The answer came to him in an instant. "The air!" he exclaimed and in a flash he removed the valve on the tire and with it released the crushing pressure that was pinning Phillip's leg.

In less than a minute, Phillip was free. George gently hoisted him over his shoulder and started briskly toward the station wagon, Phillip's left leg dangling lifelessly next to his chest. "Betty, go into the clinic and call ahead to the hospital! I can feel his leg crepitate below the knee," he called over his shoulder. I knew what that meant from working in the clinic. There was an obvious break where the bones had snapped below the knee, and George could feel them rubbing together with each stride. Phillip, meanwhile, was moaning dismally with each step.

After I called the hospital, George said "Get the station wagon. It'll be faster if you drive!"

I ran back into the house to get the keys while George laid Phillip in the back seat and sat next to him. Allen and

Doyle stood by the side of the car, watching anxiously.

"Allen, stay with Doyle," I called out as we drove down the driveway and pulled out onto the highway. I looked through the rearview mirror and could see him trying to comfort his distraught brother on the front lawn.

"Surely you have borne our grief and carried our sorrows . . ." I began saying to myself softly, even as George was trying to comfort Phillip in the back seat. "And by your stripes, Lord, we are healed!"

"Phillip?" I looked up as we sped toward Middle Tennessee Hospital on University Avenue, "Start saying Isaiah 53." He knew that verse as well as we did. So George and I tried to encourage him to speak it out.

But you were wounded for our transgressions; you were bruised for our iniquities; the chastisement for our peace was upon you, and by your stripes we are healed.

When we arrived at the hospital, a team of doctors was waiting. They placed Phillip on a gurney and began examining him, even as they wheeled him off for an X-ray. "Get a splint!" the emergency room doctor said, and a couple of nurses responded.

And with that Phillip was wheeled away from us through a series of double doors to the X-ray room beyond.

In a few minutes the doctors came back. Phillip looked much calmer and in far less pain. I waited anxiously to hear the news.

"Nothing's broken," said the doctor, shaking his head. "It's unbelievable, really!"

George lifted his hands into the air. "Praise God!" he exclaimed, catching us all by surprise. The doctors looked at him, stunned, visibly moved by his outburst of thanks.

It was evening by the time we came home to Allen and Doyle with strict instructions to soak Phillip's bruised leg in water every day and to use pressure to stretch it out flat. When we put him in the bath, he would scream in pain. Although nothing was broken, it quickly became clear that the trauma to the ligaments had left him crippled. His heel was elevated about an inch and a half from the floor, and there was a painful lesion on the back of his knee.

I knew deep down that something was wrong. Another week passed and I'd had just about as much as I could take. So I dialed a friend in Nashville, the wife of a surgeon. She listened to my brief description of Phillip's condition before interrupting me mid sentence.

"You need to change doctors, Betty," she stated bluntly.

"Take him to Dr. Ben Fowler. He's a friend of my husband's at Vanderbilt."

Two days later, we were sitting in Dr. Fowler's office as he carefully examined Phillip's leg and large lesion. "What you have been doing is causing more harm than good," he said, shaking his head and looking at the leg lesion." The leg shouldn't have been stretched like that. I'm afraid he may require surgery now. We can get him walking again, Mrs. Jackson, but it's going to take time. I need to re-examine him in two weeks," he said. "Go ahead and schedule surgery over the Christmas vacation."

For several months, we kept praying and thanking God for Phillip's healing.

A well-known Bible teacher was holding a meeting at the brand-new YMCA in Chattanooga. Since Phillip's surgery was not scheduled until the Christmas holiday, a window of opportunity appeared to open. "Perhaps we can go to the meeting and ask him to pray for Phillip," I said to George.

The following Saturday arrived and with it a beautiful two-hour drive through the string of Appalachian foothills that mark the boundaries of Tennessee, Georgia, and North Carolina, setting our watches forward an hour as we crossed the Tennessee River and entered the eastern time zone. When we got to the meeting, there were about three hundred people filling the hall, but there were still a handful of empty seats right at the front.

George led the family to the front row.

It was a simple service: a short time of worship, testimony, and prayer, followed by a message that we'd heard many times before. But it was significant nevertheless.

Therefore, I say to you, the preacher proclaimed, reading from Mark 11:24: *whatever things you ask when you pray, believe that you receive them, and you will have them.*

He paused and looked out over the crowd. "Those of you who have been believing God for a specific thing, please stand."

That was us. George and Phillip immediately stood up, and I swiftly rose to my feet to join them. We'd been praying for months for Phillip's healing. Even Doyle had taken part. Phillip stood next to me, quietly holding George's hand in obvious discomfort. Allen and Doyle were standing as well.

Phillip wept. "Daddy," he whispered to George next to me, "my knee just jumped and got all hot."

George immediately said, "God has probably healed you." George bent over and looked down at Phillip's right leg. "Betty, look!" he whispered excitedly. "His heel is on the floor!"

Just then the minister began closing the service in the prayer of faith for healing. "Father God," he called out, "You are the God that moves mountains. You are the God Who answers prayer. We depend upon You, Lord. We trust in You completely. Forgive their sins and heal their bodies, in the mighty name of Jesus I pray!"

It was dark by the time we began driving back home, past Lookout Mountain, across Nickajack Lake, and through the fertile river plain of the Sequatchie Valley. One by one the boys fell asleep in the back of the station wagon, while George and I reflected on the dramatic picture we'd seen—watching God perform the impossible before our very eyes. It was amazing. It was exhilarating. But it was also a little overwhelming. And there was still a lingering feeling of doubt. Was Phillip's leg *really* healed?

For days afterward, I would watch him out of the kitchen window, riding his bike in the driveway as before, and sometimes that same small feeling of doubt would start creeping back in. Was the miracle real, or were we imagining it? So I would step outside and wait for him to dismount, just to see if he was truly walking with his foot flat on the ground. And then I remembered the verse from Mark 11 the preacher read in Chattanooga: . . . *whatever things you ask when you pray, believe that you receive them, and you will have them.*

"I'm sorry, Lord, for doubting You," I would say as I stepped back into the house.

• • •

THE SUMMER OF 1969 passed quickly in a whirr of activity. The weekend after Phillip's healing, we found ourselves gathered round the television set in our living room, at nine-thirty on a Sunday night, watching Neil Armstrong prepare to take man's first steps on the moon. Doyle had fallen asleep some hours earlier, but the older boys were determined to stay up and watch history unfold. Even I was drawn in, transfixed by the drama of the spectacle as the epic moon mission of Apollo 11 reached a thrilling conclusion.

It was early November and I was working at my desk in the clinic fielding calls for George. To my surprise a call came inviting us to take a trip to Israel, only this time it was to make an investment in the boys.

I was shocked at the thought. Barely a year had passed since our first trip, and neither of us expected another invitation to come so soon. Besides, the timing wasn't particularly convenient. Doyle was still too young to appreciate Israel, and he would need to be cared for all the time we were away. Allen and Phillip, meanwhile, would have to miss three weeks of school. And that wasn't so easy, now that Allen was in Junior High.

Aside from the show season in late summer, spring was George's busiest time. Brood mares were in foal by the dozen in the pasture behind the clinic and in breeding farms right across the state. And Dr. Jackson was in constant demand. "It's hardly a good time for me. But I think the time is right. Why wouldn't we invest in them? I think we should take them!"

And that was that. Once George made up his mind, there was no turning back.

We were well into January before we had finalized the details, but they all came together quite remarkably in the end. My sister Glenda and her husband would watch Doyle in Missouri, while George's assistant would stay and look after the farm. Clients were informed and arrangements made for their horses to be cared for in our absence. But George still worked harder than ever in the months leading up to the tour, going the extra mile to make sure that each client would have reason to seek out his services as soon as the clinic reopened in May.

We joined a twenty-two day tour to Italy, Israel, Switzerland and England. Before we knew it, we found ourselves approaching Tel Aviv, coming in to land in Israel for the second time in less than two years.

It was late afternoon and there was a festive atmosphere on the plane. The men in our group were all wearing suits or light sport coats, while the women were in dresses and high heels. Both Allen and Phillip had their faces pressed against a window, wide-eyed with anticipation.

The next day we stopped by a shallow inlet on the Sea of Galilee, just north of Tiberius. Several members of the group were asking to be baptized. And there was Phillip, standing in their midst, watching and listening to every word they were saying.

"May I?" he said simply, looking up at Derek.

"What was that Phillip?" he replied, stooping down to give him his full attention.

"May I get baptized here too?" Derek glanced over at George who nodded in agreement.

"Of course you can young man!"

The days passed quickly and we relived our earlier

trip, this time with a different focus. We were making an investment in the children.

It was our last day in Jerusalem. We began at the Garden Tomb, close to our hotel, and began exploring the Old City, from St. Anne's and the Pools of Bethesda, all the way to the ancient Church of the Holy Sepulcher in the heart of the Christian Quarter. The boys did their best to keep up and take it all in, but I could tell that so much of it was washing over them. Then, towards the end of the afternoon we started climbing the steep hill to the top of the Mount of Olives, stopping at the Garden of Gethsemane to look at the two thousand year-old olive grove. As we did, I could tell they were becoming more alive. The gnarled trunks and branches of these ancient trees spoke so much more powerfully to them, than the rocks, and shrines and stones of the city.

As the sun was setting we made it to the top, ready to have one final group photograph overlooking Jerusalem. Before we turned to face the camera I told the boys to drink in the view, our eyes darting down the winding path, past the ancient Jewish cemetery, with ten thousands of white stone boxes seemingly carved into the side of the hill. We looked down at the Garden of Gethsemane and beyond it to the Eastern Gate, its three arches blocked shut by the Medieval Muslim ruler Suleiman, as if by doing this he could prevent Jesus' return.

We stayed on the Mount of Olives that evening, where

we experienced our first ever Passover meal, led by a Jewish believer, Shlomo Isaac. He spoke of the unleavened 'matza' bread that ever since the Egyptian Exodus has been made the same way: bruised, striped, pierced and broken, in the same way that on that greatest of Passovers, Jesus' body was broken for us. He spoke of the blood of the lamb, sprinkled on the doorposts of the Israelite homes, just as the blood of Jesus was shed on the Cross for our sins. We left that night, astonished at what we'd heard and returned to the hotel, overflowing with a sense of the goodness of God, reluctantly preparing for the long journey home.

The plan was to stop in London for a few days of sight-seeing before concluding our trip with a visit to South Chard. But it was in London that the full impact of what had taken place in Israel became clear.

It was on the second day that Derek took us to Speakers' Corner, a famous area on the edge of Hyde Park, which, for over a hundred years, had been a forum for open, public debate.

"If Paul used Mars Hill in Athens to spread the gospel," he argued, "I've never understood why more Christians don't use Speakers' Corner to tell people about Jesus, right here in the heart of the City of London."

Standing in a large circle, Derek gave the group instructions.

Much to our surprise, it was seven-year-old Phillip who stepped forward first.

"I couldn't walk," he began, confidently and clearly. "It started when my leg slipped against the tractor tire and it pulled me up and over the tire wedging my leg between the tire and fender. My leg was crippled and the doctors said I needed surgery. But we prayed and Jesus healed me!"

It was simple, but profound and I saw George, standing next to me, wiping tears.

Scan this code with your camera-equipped smartphone to view the companion video for Chapter Twelve. If you do not have the QR app on your phone, visit your app store and search for **QR code reader.**

THIRTEEN

DO YOU NEED TO FORGIVE . . . ?

*Nothing in all creation is
hidden from God's sight.*
Hebrews 4:13 (NIV1984)

We were in the middle of a dogwood winter—that period right before Easter when frigid winds sweep through the Tennessee Valley, catching the late blossoming trees unaware. Each year, it was as though the cold weather fronts would mount a last-ditch assault on spring for a week before being beaten back by summer's searing heat.

Allen was shivering when he came home from basketball practice.

"You should have taken a coat," I reminded him.

"But, Mom, it was warm this morning," he responded. It was a Friday afternoon, and the boys were all relieved to be through another week. The phone rang just as the family sat down for dinner.

"Jackson Veterinary Clinic, may I help you?"

"Betty?" The English voice was familiar, but I was

struggling to place it. "Sid Purse here. I'm visiting Tom Monroe in Indiana, and Tom has agreed to fly me to Murfreesboro to see you. Can you pick me up at the Murfreesboro airfield?"

"George," I whispered, covering the handset with one hand, and holding it up in the air in an effort to attract his attention.

"Excuse me, Uncle Sid," I said, quickly, "I'm sure it will be fine, but I just need to ask George to take your call."

"No problem!" he said, in his soft British accent.

"George, this is Sid Purse from Chard, in England. He is visiting Tom Monroe in Indiana and wants to come visit us. I think you should take the call."

"Uncle Sid?" George exclaimed. "What a nice surprise. We will be happy to have you in Murfreesboro. What time do you plan to arrive?"

"About an hour and a half," he replied.

"We look forward to seeing you then."

Allen and Phillip remembered Uncle Sid fondly from our time spent at his home and the Christian community in England we had visited while on our way home from Israel. The boys were thrilled at the thought of his arrival. They remembered the thatched roofs of the houses in the neighborhood where we stayed when we made our visit to Chard, south of London.

"I'm amazed he remembered us," said George. "It's quite an honor that he would come."

Before leaving for the airport, we recalled the words of a friend in reference to the Christians in Chard: "If I had a choice of a place where I could be when Jesus returns, I would choose to be with the Congregation of Sid Purse." Uncle Sid was the much-loved senior pastor of a large group, and he also traveled around Europe, where he ministered personally to many believers.

I quickly reminded the boys of the story of a little girl in that congregation who had prayed for a "Green Pram" [doll buggy] at Christmas time. She had wanted a green one, but her parents were unable to find a green one, so they purchased the only one they could find. The pram's box said it was blue, but on Christmas morning, when the little girl opened her gift, the pram was green, just what she had prayed for.

It was dark by the time George returned from the airport. Uncle Sid was a small man, about five-foot-five and fairly thin. He was soft-spoken and very kind. He must have been in his late sixties in those days, a true English gentleman whom you would be hard-pressed to find wearing anything but a suit.

"Uncle Sid. It's so good to see you." We were surprised that he would remember us, as we were among a large group of Americans and we had a very small amount of personal time with him.

We heard about his ministry in England and his visit in Indiana, where plans were unfolding to establish a TV tower in South Florida for the spread of the gospel. After a good cup of English tea, Uncle Sid and the family settled down for a night of rest.

The next morning, he emerged from the room soon after we awoke.

"What about breakfast?" I asked, as I served him a cup of tea.

"No. I'm fasting." He sat down in the living room, his Bible in his lap, and stayed there most of the morning.

"How's Auntie Mill?" I asked. Auntie Mill, Sid's wife, had been so gracious to us and had made us feel so welcome when we visited their home, and we understood that she stayed at home while he traveled. They worked as a team, and their unselfishness was evident to all who knew them.

"Mill is just fine; she sends her love. Tell me, where is George?"

"He begins his day by checking the horses that are patients in the clinic. He will return to the house once he has finished. Uncle Sid, would you like me to call some friends and invite them to hear you speak while you are here? We have a Bible study in our home, and I'm sure they would love to come over, perhaps tomorrow night, meet you, and perhaps you would share with them?"

"No, it's fine," Uncle Sid replied simply.

Around lunchtime, George strode into the kitchen. "George," I said, "go and ask Uncle Sid if he wants lunch?"

"No, he will fast through lunch but will have dinner with us. Sid says that he has been introduced to Kentucky Fried Chicken and he was favorably impressed."

At dinner time we were all sitting around the table with fried chicken, coleslaw, and lukewarm mashed potatoes, picking up pieces of battered fried chicken in our hands. And Uncle Sid loved it.

"This is a real treat!" he exclaimed, taking his third piece of chicken. "Thank you!"

"Don't you have fried chicken in England?" asked Doyle, thoroughly enjoying the experience but a little perplexed all the same.

"No, son," Sid answered, a glint in his eye, "just fish and chips!"

I stood up to clear the table, busying myself in the kitchen while the boys listened intently to George and Uncle Sid recounting our family trip to Israel and our time spent in England.

"Are you sure you wouldn't like to speak to our Bible study?" George asked as they remained seated at the yellow kitchen table. "They would love to meet you…"

"No. No. George, that's not why I'm here. . . . So why am I here? For your family, for your marriage. No one else." He then shared with us that George had given him a business card while we sat at dinner with him one evening and told him at that time that we, along with a large group of Americans, were fasting and praying one day each week for our nation. He said simply, "I never could forget that you told me as a family you were fasting and praying." And with that he stood up, walked into the bedroom, and returned to the living room with a little notebook and pencil in hand. He opened it to the first clean page and wrote George's name. Then he underlined it. I went about my work in the kitchen. George went to sit opposite him on the couch.

"Now. When did you first become interested in animals, George?"

"From the time I was young, growing up. I spent a lot of time with my mother's parents. Even after my dad remarried, I would still go there—during the holidays and over the summer. My grandfather always had a pony for me to ride and one or two milk cows. They had a small farm at the edge of the community, and I guess I made friends with the animals as a young boy. I didn't have siblings there, but many friends."

"What was your childhood like, George?" Uncle Sid looked down on the page, ready to write. George hesitated. He barely talked about it with me, and I had never heard him discuss it with other people.

"My mother died when I was eight days old," he started cautiously. "So I lived with her parents the first two years of my life."

"What then?" Sid prompted.

"Well, my father married a college friend of my mother's, and they wanted me to come live with them. So of course I did."

"Do you have any memory of that?"

George shook his head. "Except . . ." George wiped the back of his hand across his face, clearly uncomfortable with what he was sharing. "I spent summers and holidays with my grandparents. And each time I would leave, I would cry. When I got home I would go straight to my room and keep crying for several hours until I went to sleep."

"How old were you?"

"I don't know. I think that went on until I was perhaps fourteen."

George talked freely. Uncle Sid made notes. "I remember as a very small boy, Cleo, my new mother, holding my hand through the bars of the crib while I went to sleep at night. My mother's picture was never allowed on my dresser. When I would put it out, I would always find it back in the drawer. Dad was tense, and I always wondered if I was the cause; had I done something wrong?"

That was as far as they got that night. The phone rang: a brood mare was having difficulty with labor on a farm out in Eagleville. George apologized hurriedly and left. Uncle Sid closed his notebook and went to bed.

It was mid-morning Monday before he picked it up again. The boys were back at school, breakfast was cleaned away, and George was already back from his first two morning calls. Uncle Sid had been in his room, fasting once again.

"Do you have a minute?" Uncle Sid inquired as George stepped into the kitchen. He had come out of the bedroom just a few minutes earlier and taken up residence in his favorite living room chair. "I want to talk to you about rejection," he said.

"Sure," said George, reluctantly. "But I don't think that's my issue. You see, I was never rejected. My dad went to every football and basketball game I played . . ."

"His dad has always been good to me," I interjected, coming to George's defense. "He's always shown us a lot of love."

"George, let me explain," Uncle Sid replied. "When we're born, we're designed by God to be loved and accepted, to be held in our parents' arms. Being held in the strong arms of your parents is very important. Every baby craves this kind of security. And if you don't get it, you may grow up with an inability to be loved or to give love. Often it will affect every relationship in your life—*especially* your marriage."

"Well, I have felt alone and isolated at times, I guess," George conceded. "And I certainly felt *more* accepted by my grandparents. I was their only survivor. They were respected in the community and always seemed proud of me as their grandson."

Uncle Sid was blunt in response. "It is possible that you felt rejection, George," he said simply.

Suddenly, I saw a pained look dart across George's eyes. He sat down slowly on the couch.

"Jesus understands your pain," Sid continued. "He will help you forgive those who have rejected you."

"My parents?" George questioned.

"You know those who reject us rarely intend to," Uncle Sid said gently. "More often than not it comes down to circumstances that they have no other option; they suffer too. Rejection is painful and difficult to face. A need for forgiveness is not uppermost in one's mind, but it is the key to freedom. Freedom to love and to be loved by God, and by those close to you."

George didn't argue or protest. He simply knelt where he was by the side of the couch and prayed a simple prayer forgiving his father for going to Oregon when his mother died and leaving him with his grandparents. It was two years before he returned and decided to remarry.

"You also need to forgive your mother," Uncle Sid calmly suggested.

"My mother?" said George.

"She died and left you, too; it was not her choice," Sid explained.

"I feel like I have a basketball in my stomach," George said quietly. Uncle Sid just sat there, quiet, patiently sitting in his chair. A few moments later, George was quiet, kneeling with his head up and eyes closed. "God, you know I forgive my mother." Minutes passed without a sound in the room.

"Now God can heal you, George. Your Heavenly Father offers you total acceptance through Jesus—*His* beloved Son, just as it says in the Scriptures:

> *having predestined us to adoption as sons by Jesus Christ to Himself, according to the good pleasure of His will, to the praise of the glory of His grace, by which He made us accepted in the Beloved.*
> (Ephesians 1:5–6)

"Healing comes when we know we are a part of *God's* family. When we accept *Him* as our father and when we understand that Jesus was willing to be rejected Himself, so we can share in His inheritance, His acceptance, and His adoption!"

Over the course of the following nights, Uncle Sid continued to spend time with the two of us, and we both in turn spent a lot of time by the couch on our knees! So we learned knowledge won't bring healing. Telling our stories and retelling our past won't bring healing. Rehashing all our family disappointments and our failures—it doesn't bring healing to our hearts and minds.

There were areas of our past we had stuffed deep inside, and the emotional pain was stifling our present. In some areas of our relationship, we were failures. We needed restoration. We needed God's forgiveness, and we needed to forgive each other. The following days the three of us talked together. We went back over our lives from early childhood, sharing both good and bad experiences, crying and laughing together as we covered the years.

Before we knew it, a week had passed and it was time for Uncle Sid to move on. It was only at the time of his departure the following Friday that we realized he had been cold from fasting. Some nights he slept in his suit.

"You are smoother stones now, Betty," Uncle Sid remarked as he left for the airport. "You have both had good grinders." He winked at George as he climbed into the station wagon.

I went immediately to the clinic to spend the day bringing the records up to date. I was grateful to our Heavenly Father—still amazed deep inside that God had sent Uncle Sid. For the first time in our married life, it truly felt like there was nothing hidden between us. Everything was in the light. It was an experience we could never have bought or paid for.

Three o'clock came around. I needed information on one more posting to close the accounts for the week. At the end of every day, George was supposed to transfer his billing notes to mine. But he often got busy, distracted, or forgot.

"George, could you transfer your last treatment?" I asked. "You only lack one."

"I'll get to it," he mumbled, lost in something else.

About an hour later, he still hadn't done it.

"George, you still haven't given me the information I need."

"I've been busy, Betty. I'll do it!" he snapped. And before we knew it, we were arguing again. "Guess Uncle Sid's visit didn't make so much difference after all!" I thought. I dialed the number he had left us.

"Uncle Sid. It's just like before. We are arguing the same way we did before you came!"

I heard his soft laugh at the other end of the phone. "Betty," he said, "I'm not surprised. It's just the enemy seeking to rob you. Recognize where it's coming from and take authority over it. The Lord has done a great work in you. Trust Him in it!"

"Oh!" I said, not quite knowing what else to say. I passed the phone to George so he could hear it as well.

"Don't let division come back in," Uncle Sid warned. "Forgive each other. Keep short accounts."

George and I looked at each other, joined hands immediately, and prayed. The tension left us and peace came back. Uncle Sid was right, the Lord had done a great work in us, and as the days progressed, we noticed it more and more. Our marriage was changed. We seemed to be working together in greater unity. And that's the truth—Uncle Sid's visit was indeed a gift that could not be bought or paid for. Our spiritual lives had changed, and it was for the good.

Scan this code with your camera-equipped smartphone to view the companion video for Chapter Thirteen. If you do not have the QR app on your phone, visit your app store and search for *QR code reader.*

FOURTEEN

WE OVERCOME!

And they overcame him by the blood of the Lamb and by the word of their testimony, and they did not love their lives to the death.
Revelation 12:11

I got a call from my younger sister Glenda. She sounded distressed.

"What is it, Glenda?" I asked, noticing the concern evident in her voice.

"It's Dorothy," she replied. "They denied her surgery in Tulsa. The doctors said there was nothing they could do!" For many years, my older sister Dorothy had been suffering with a serious heart condition, but it was becoming clear she had exhausted all medical options. As I was in the midst of my own ongoing struggle against cancer, it was beginning to feel like we were losing ground on every side.

"How is she handling it?" I asked.

"She's discouraged. And the pain is getting worse."

"I'll talk to George," I told her. "Maybe I can fly out to see her—perhaps even next week. Isn't it her wedding anniversary then?"

It was a Friday night in early March when I arrived at my parents' house in Sarcoxie, after flying from Nashville to Springfield. It was such a joy to see my parents, and it became obvious that mother believed Dorothy's health would improve; there was no question in her mind. The next day they took me on the short forty-mile drive past Joplin and across the state line to Baxter Springs, Kansas, where Dorothy's husband, John, pastored a small congregation.

It was always good to be together with Dorothy and John. We shared stories from their early married life, when my brother Doyle and I were still at home: composing poetry for family gatherings; sleigh rides behind John's car on the ice-packed roads of South Missouri; trips to Kansas City to visit them in their first apartment. And in the midst of the laughter and the memories, I spent time cleaning Dorothy's house, washing the windows, and doing the things that she herself had not been able to manage for quite some time, singing to myself and chatting with Dorothy as I did. It was such a joy!

The final night of my stay was the evening of their twenty-fifth wedding anniversary. So I worked hard all day and prepared a beautiful candlelit dinner for the three of us. Afterwards, we sat in the living room and listened to a cassette tape of Evelyn Simpson singing "His Eye Is on the Sparrow." It was one of my favorite songs, and Dorothy had asked me to play it after the conversation turned to the time she had visited our home in Murfreesboro and met the Simpsons for the first time.

> *Why should I be discouraged,*
>   *why should the shadows fall?*
> *Why should my heart grow weary*
>   *and long for Heaven and Home?*
> *When Jesus is my portion,*
>   *my constant friend is He.*
> *His eye is on a sparrow,*
>   *and I know He watches me!*
> *His eye is on a sparrow,*
>   *and I know He watches me!*

Dorothy loved music and had always loved to sing. And as Evelyn sang the line "Why should my heart grow weary and long for Heaven and Home," I saw her face change. I knew God had made something real to her. My thoughts turned to the day I lay in that hospital bed in Columbia, having been told that I only had six months to live. It was Dorothy who reached into my life that day, with the words of a simple get-well card:

> *For He who put the stars in place*
> *And rules the land and sea,*
> *It's such a loving little task*
> *To care for you and me!*

Our situations were different, but the message was the same.

As the plane taxied onto the rain-swept runway the following afternoon, I felt peace about Dorothy, as I had not forgotten the expression on her face as Evelyn sang, *When Jesus is my portion, my constant friend is He, His eye is on a sparrow, and I know He watches me!*

In the stillness of that half-empty airplane, I had time to go back over the past few years of my own life. After the 1965 "clean bill of health" at Mayo Clinic, I lived free of the threat of cancer. In 1970, when Doyle was five years old, the lumps appeared again. I entered the Miller Clinic in Nashville for surgery; the diagnosis was simply, "diseased tissue."

The following day, after I arrived back home, Dorothy called. "Betty, the most amazing thing happened after you left." There was an excitement in her voice that traveled through the line.

"John was gone, so I took a bath—the first time I have been strong enough to do that on my own since . . . I don't know when. Once I got out, I washed my hair, got dressed, and started walking through the house. Then I saw my accordion behind the sofa. You know, Betty, I probably haven't touched it in two years—maybe more. So I picked it up . . ."

"That heavy instrument?" I asked, surprised. Dorothy hadn't been strong enough to lift anything but the lightest of weights for many months.

"Yes!" she said, not thinking of the months just past. "I strapped it on and began to walk through the house singing and playing. I was thinking of our grandparents and uncles and aunts—what it would be like to see them in heaven for myself. And suddenly I realized that I'll see Jesus! It was so exciting. I'll see him Betty. And no sooner had that thought come to mind that I felt this distinct movement in my chest. The pain lifted, and all of a sudden I feel so free!"

I could think of little else throughout the weeks and months that followed. Dorothy, it turned out, had been completely healed. But it only happened when she yielded her will. I did not fully grasp what had happened to Dorothy.

But I wasn't there yet. I had so many desires—good desires, godly desires. I wanted to be with George, and I did not want the boys to be without a mother.

Suddenly I remembered a chapter called *The Prayer of Relinquishment* in one of Catherine Marshall's books.

The Lord was trying to teach me, and time after time I would find myself back staring at the pages of Luke 9:23–24:

> *Then he said to them all: "If anyone would come after me, he must deny himself and take up his cross daily and follow me. For whoever wants to save his life will lose it, but whoever loses his life for me will save it."* (NIV 1984)

It was a painful process. Slowly, I understood that my will had to go and I had to choose His. For Dorothy and for Catherine Marshall, the pathway to healing was nothing less than total surrender. But what did that surrender look like for me? I found myself getting down on my face night after night and crying out to God, sometimes into the early hours of the morning.

"Heavenly Father, I'm a rebellious person, please help me. My will is so far from Yours. I want to know You."

• • •

IN MY HEART of hearts I trusted the Lord. And the more I tried to encourage others in their struggles, I was very much aware that I was fighting for my own life. Yes, my symptoms weren't getting any worse, but what did that really mean? So many times I had seen people enjoy months, even years, of remission, only to waste away in a few short months as the dormant cancer cells began ravaging their bodies once more.

Would I face such a crisis also?

Upon returning from a trip out of town, I emptied the mail from our overflowing mailbox, and my eyes fell on a handwritten note from a local church across town.

"George, there's another invitation for you to show one of Derek's teaching videos here in Murfreesboro," I said as I began sorting through the rest of the correspondence on my desk back in the clinic. Over the previous year, our Christian outreach of *Disciples Inc.* had steadily grown, as a steady stream of churches began inviting George to share some of the video teaching materials we were gradually accumulating on a range of topics and issues.

"When do they want me to come?" he asked.

I stopped what I was doing and looked back at the letter. "I guess he means tomorrow!"

"Phone them and check, would you?" George asked as he began walking out the door. "I would be happy to do it. I think I'll take that message on the blood of Jesus."

I was quiet.

George paused in the doorway and turned back. "You know, Betty, I just think that if people could grasp all that Jesus did on the Cross, their lives would change."

I wasn't sure I wanted to go.

The next day came. Reluctantly, I agreed to go to the meeting, for George's sake more than anything else. But while he went to the front of the sanctuary and connected the video to the television monitor, I just sat on the back pew. It was all I could do to be there. In fact, I was in one of the lowest places in my life. I had stood on the Scriptures, I had fasted and I had prayed, and I had seen God work in many other people's lives. But I had also seen a few too many of them die. I was beginning to lose hope. . . .

"Sometimes we think that the blood of Jesus is just a topic for Good Friday," George began, standing at the front of the church. "But I have learned that what Jesus did for us affects our whole lives.

"Derek's teaching is centered on the Exodus story and its connection to Jesus' sacrifice on the Cross. When God delivered the Jewish people out of Egyptian slavery, He told them to kill a lamb, to take its blood and put it in a basin. Then He instructed them to go out in the field and find a bunch of hyssop with which to smear the blood over the doorposts of their homes. It was the blood of that lamb that ensured that the angel of death would "pass over" the Israelites and spare their children. But for the blood to save them, it had to be transferred from the basin to the door."

George continued, "Paul says in 1 Corinthians, chapter 5 that *'Christ, our Passover, has been sacrificed for us,'* just as Derek will tell you on the grainy, black and white, reel-to-reel tape. He has been killed. His blood has been shed. When we think in terms of the Exodus story, His blood is now in the basin. But the basin does nothing for you or for me. We have to transfer the blood from the basin to the place where we are—to our personal need: spiritual, physical, financial, family, business. Whatever it may be, we have to get the blood of Jesus out of the basin and to where we live—to our address. And God has provided the means. Of course, it is not hyssop or any other herb we might find growing in the fields. What is it? It is by our testimony that we transfer the blood from the basin to the door. As it says in Revelation 12 verse 11:

> *And they overcame him by the blood of the Lamb*
> *and by the word of their testimony, and they did*
> *not love their lives to the death.*

Within a few minutes, the video began. I had pulled out a notebook and was outlining, point-by-point, all the things that Jesus' death had done for me. For the first time in my life, I saw the Blood of Jesus as a weapon—a weapon of atomic proportions—that could defeat the power of sin, sickness, and death. The more Derek spoke, the more I understood that what George had just told us was absolutely true!

Faith was rising in me as we left the church that night, the message of the blood of Jesus was becoming personal to me. I stayed up late into the night typing out my notes, and from those drew a prayer of confession that I could say each day, to apply the redemptive work of Jesus' blood to my situation. In the morning, I made one copy to send to Derek and another to post on the tile wall next to my bathtub. I finally realized that I had a weapon against the enemy. But it was up to me to use it:

BY THE BLOOD OF THE LAMB AND THE WORD OF MY TESTIMONY,

I OVERCOME THE DEVIL

> Revelation 12:11—*"And they overcame him by the blood of the Lamb and by the word of their testimony, and they did not love their lives to the death."*

I, Betty Jackson testify to Satan personally as to what the Word of God says the Blood of Jesus does for me.

> Ephesians 1:7—*"In whom we have redemption through his blood, the forgiveness of sins according to the riches of his grace."*

> Psalm 107:2—*"Let the Redeemed of the Lord say so, whom He has redeemed from the hand of the enemy."*

Through the blood of Jesus, I am redeemed out of the hand of the devil.

Through the blood of Jesus, all of my sins are forgiven.

> I John 1:7—*"But if we walk in the light, as he [Jesus] is in the light, we have fellowship with one another, and the blood of Jesus Christ, God's Son, cleanses us from all sin."*

The blood of Jesus Christ, God's Son, continually cleanses me from all sin.

Romans 5:9— *"Since we have been justified by His blood, how much more shall we be saved from wrath through Him!"* (NIV)

Through the blood of Jesus, I am justified, made righteous, just as if I'd never sinned.

Hebrews 13:12— *"Therefore Jesus also, that he might sanctify the people with his own blood, suffered without the gate."*

Through the blood of Jesus, I am sanctified, made holy set apart to God.

1 Corinthians 6:13b— *"Now the body is not for sexual immorality but for the Lord, and the Lord for the body."*

1 Corinthians 6:19–20— *"Do you not know that your body is a temple of the Holy Spirit who is in you, whom you have from God and you are not your own? For you were bought at a price; therefore glorify God in your body and in your spirit, which are God's."*

> My body is a temple of the Holy Spirit, redeemed,
> cleansed, sanctified by the blood of Jesus.
>
> THEREFORE, BECAUSE OF ALL THAT'S GONE BEFORE,
> SATAN HAS NO PLACE IN ME . . . NO POWER OVER ME
> THROUGH THE BLOOD OF JESUS CHRIST I RENOUNCE HIM,
> LOOSE MYSELF FROM HIM, AND COMMAND HIM TO LEAVE ME
> IN THE NAME OF JESUS.

During the weeks and months that followed, I kept repeating this prayer when I was alone in the bathtub, while working in the clinic, or when driving in the car to the grocery store. I memorized the Scripture verses, declaring this profound prayer of confession aloud.

This went on for several weeks, and my faith increased. Yet soon it was again tested, this time by a friend in need. It was an early evening in June, and I stole a few minutes to myself to check on my roses growing around the patio before serving dinner and getting the boys to bed. The fireflies were out in full force, their bright neon bodies flashing like beacons in the fading half-light. My friend called shortly after I stepped back into the house. "Betty, do you have a moment?"

"Of course. What's wrong?"

"Betty, I just received the results of a positive pap smear," her voice was faltering on the other end of the phone.

"Oh," I exclaimed, "I'm so sorry!"

I got off the phone aching inside with grief. I knew how much her children needed their mother, how much her husband valued his wife.

"Lord, heal her," I cried, wiping the tears from my eyes.

Ten o'clock came round, and I slipped into bed. George was already fast asleep, but my mind was racing. If the blood of Jesus was sufficient for me, it was sufficient for my friend.

I got up and went back into the den, as far away as I could, hoping not to disturb George or the boys, and sat down on the floor. I began softly to praise the Lord. I felt praise for the Lord rising from my heart for His greatness that He put the stars into place and He knows the number of hairs on my head. I went back to bed, but my attitude of praise continued the rest of the night. God's greatness became more and more real to me. It was near morning before I dropped off to sleep.

The next afternoon my friend called again.

"Betty, you'll never believe it!"

"What?" I said.

"The doctor called and told me there had been a mistake. Apparently I don't have cancer after all." I thought back to my journey to Mayo Clinic all those years earlier. I knew for myself that sometimes we miss the greatest miracles in our lives. When God doesn't act, we blame Him bitterly, but when He intervenes we're so quick to explain it away. But I knew He had intervened for my friend.

And, in that moment, I knew He could intervene for me.

At bath time late that evening, still awed by the sense of God's presence filling the house all around me, I began running the hot water into the tub.

"Lord, I thank you for my friend," I prayed. "I know you changed her destiny."

I sank down into the warm water and looked up to where I had posted the blood of Jesus' confession on the white tile on the far wall. I knew it had changed me, deep within. I knew that proclaiming it day after day had strengthened my faith and given me hope. Without thought, I leaned forward and heard myself say to Jesus as though He were in the room with me. "I want to tell you something. I love you more than George; I love you more than the boys; I love you more than my own life. I want to do whatever you want me to do. If you want me to die of cancer, then that is exactly what I want. I want to come to be with you."

I stood up and put a towel around me. I knew I had won the battle.

That very week a friend recommended that I visit a well-known gynecologist in Nashville, Dr. Robert Chala-fant—a kind man in his late fifties with a lot of experience who put me instantly at ease.

"Tell me your story, Mrs. Jackson," he began.

I stared at him for a moment, not sure where exactly to begin. "My story?" I tried my best, as briefly as I could, giving him a sense of my journey from Doyle's birth and the diagnosis in Columbia, the trip to Mayo Clinic, and the return of lumps. "Let me take a look," he said after a few further questions.

Soon afterward, he and the nurse both left the room. In a few minutes they came back with a tray. "This will just take a minute."

Before I knew anything had happened, the doctor took off his gloves with a triumphant look on his face.

"There's the lump, Mrs. Jackson! You can get dressed now."

Very soon, both the doctor and his nurse returned to the room, and after a brief explanation, he handed me a prescription. "Yes. I believe we have solved your problem. I believe it is hormonal." I took only one of the pills and thankfully he was right. It's been almost forty years.

Scan this code with your camera-equipped smartphone to view the companion video for Chapter Fourteen. If you do not have the QR app on your phone, visit your app store and search for *QR code reader.*

EPILOGUE

We are now well into the twenty-first century. Our lives and world have changed a great deal since those days at Mayo Clinic . . . despair yielded to purpose, fear was overcome by trust and the pursuit of God filled our lives.

Standing on the promenade overlooking Jerusalem from the South I realize we have lived an improbable story. But then following God is not about routine. Abraham had understood this when he traveled toward Mount Moriah, Jerusalem's temple mount, with Isaac. He had very likely had a glimpse of the area from very near our current vantage point.

The past thirty years have provided many experiences of the faithfulness of God. There was no way to anticipate all God would do when we began our journey as Christ followers…kneeling in Bud and Dot's living room and making a profession of faith. "God I am a sinner and I need a savior", I never imagined words could have such authority to transform a life. There was no way to grasp the power of repentance. Obedience to the simple truths of God had provided a momentum for a new life.

In the intervening years God has done more than we ever imagined. *Disciples, Inc.* our simple initiative to share bible teaching through video tape led to the planting of an interdenominational church. A Congregation that began with twenty-nine people now includes a two hundred acre campus, thousands in weekly worship and is involved with ministry around the globe.

Our three sons are all engaged in pastoral ministry, serving thriving congregations in Tennessee and Ohio. George and I divide our time between Tennessee and Jerusalem. In Israel we serve in a variety of roles… counselor, support for Christian social service providers, overseers of translations teams making Christian literature available to Hebrew speakers, tour hosts for many who visit the land of Israel… but mostly we pray. Our life experience has convinced us of the power of a living God and the remarkable privilege of joining God's purposes in the earth.

When we began our journey we had "everything a couple could desire." We were successful in our chosen careers, our family was healthy and growing, we had earned degrees from respected universities, we had friends to enjoy life with…yet a sense of being incomplete persisted.

When we were introduced to Jesus, as a person,

everything began to realign. I now realize our conversion was the watershed. When we made the simple profession of faith we were birthed into the Kingdom of God, a new life had begun. It took years for me to realize I would have to appropriate God's provision one lesson at a time. Being a Christ follower was not simply the recitation of a prayer and joining a church, it has been a life filled with becoming…a life directed at allowing the character of Christ to be more fully formed in me. Jesus had told the truth, *"unless a kernel of wheat falls to the ground and dies, it remains only a single seed. But if it dies, it produces many seeds."* (John 12:24)

The unfolding revelation of God in our lives may be understood in three arenas: the realization that people have great value in God's sight and we have good news to share; the necessity of a vital and effective Church; and the unfolding purposes of God for the Jewish people and the land of Israel.

The Value of People

When God's grace touched our lives we had zeal and little knowledge. What did emerge quickly was the awareness that the God perspective we had gained was too important to keep to ourselves. We have spent decades sharing our God story with people. Many have received, others have chosen to walk another path but the grace of God continues to transform people and lift them from lives of despair and despondency to places of hope and purpose.

A consistent lesson through these years is the sovereignty of God. Often we are not able to identify those who will choose to cooperate with God. Our responsibility is to share the truth we have been entrusted with. The realization that each person has a unique dignity because they are created in God's image has led us to many improbable places. Our lives have been filled with people from many nations, social settings, and widely divergent backgrounds. In every instance, those who receive the good news of Jesus experience the transforming power of God.

We have discovered great delight and purpose in serving the unlikely, caring for the broken and unashamedly inviting the powerful to embrace Jesus as Lord. Every person has a need for purpose greater than themselves; only Jesus can adequately address that fundamental need of humanity.

The Importance of Church

George and I were church attendees from childhood.

What we did not realize was that attendance and membership were not the objective.

I believe the need for a vital, effective Church has never been greater. Our world is staggering towards chaos and confusion with little sense of direction; only the truth of a living God can provide illumination in the darkness that is gathering.

In America, the revolutions of the 1960's initiated a momentum that has taken us farther and farther away from the principles of God. Our affluence and freedoms have been used to promote personal liberty and indulgence rather than to acknowledge the existence of a living God and our responsibility to Him as citizens of both earthly and heavenly realms. In the name of inclusivity Jesus has been pushed farther and farther from the public consciousness. Expressions of tolerance, diversity and inclusivity have resulted in great intolerance for Christianity. The Church is God's instrument in the earth.

If we are to see America regain momentum and shake off the addled confusion which seems to grip us, the change must begin within the Church. Our hope for the future does not reside in Washington, DC or with political parties. The possibility of change begins in the hearts of God's people. A spirit of humility and repentance is needed. We will have to lay aside our sectarian bickering and rekindle a passion for Jesus as Christ, Lord and King. For too long we have behaved as the Laodicean church described in the book of Revelation, saying "we are rich and in need of little" when in fact we are in a "pitiful" position of great need.

The Church is tasked by our Lord with being a light in the darkness. It is not fruitful to rage against the darkness. It is far more effective to increase the light. Our primary allegiance is to our Lord Jesus. We can be His unrelenting advocates in our homes, communities, businesses and schools. We serve a God of hope. The Church is not a collection of perfect people, rather a place where broken people can find hope and restoration through the redemptive work of Jesus of Nazareth.

The Unfolding Story of Israel

The tiny nation of Israel remains at the center of world attention. When we first visited Israel in 1968, it was impossible to imagine the barren hills and small cities would be transformed into the high tech, flourishing nation of modern Israel. The twisting dusty roads have been transformed into busy thoroughfares. A people who for centuries were forbidden to own property and were driven from nation after nation have become agricultural leaders for the world.

Yet the pressure on Israel grows with each passing day. The pages of God's Word provide enough insight that we should not be surprised at Israel's emergence or the increasing pressure. These trends will continue to increase. Logic would suggest the hatred and anti-Semitism that led to the holocaust would be lessons learned and never repeated. The great forces that shape our destiny are not logical but spiritual. The spiritual force given expression in the horrors of the holocaust still thrives in the earth. Thus we see new and aggressive presentations of hatred and anti-Semitism directed at the Jewish people and Israel.

God's attentiveness and His promises have not diminished. We have progressed in His timeline. The regathering of the Jewish people which began with the twentieth century will continue. The vitality of Israel will not be diminished by the threats of the annihilation or the unified resistance of the international community.

God's message for humanity is inextricably woven through the history of the Jewish people. God's future plans for His people will be made evident in His presence in the midst of the Jewish people. We have a responsibility to pray for the peace of Jerusalem and to be a comfort to the Jewish people.

AN
extra ORDINARY
LIFE

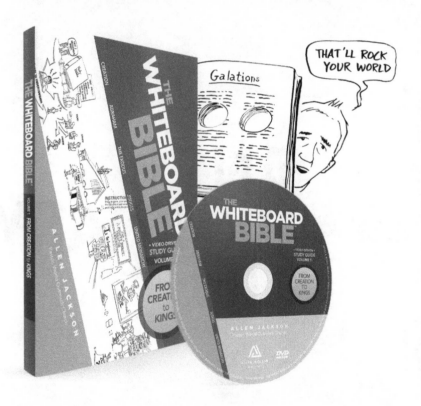

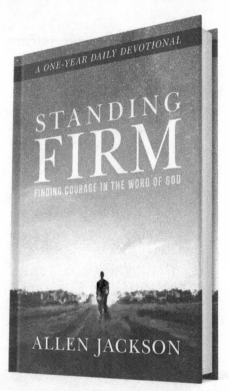